English Language Learners
in Literacy Workshops

D1361894

NCTE Editorial Board

Jonathan Bush

Barry Gilmore

Sue Hum

Claude Mark Hurlbert

Franki Sibberson

Mariana Souto-Manning

Melanie Sperling

Diane Waff

Shelbie Witte

Kurt Austin, Chair, ex officio

Kent Williamson, ex officio

Bonny Graham, ex officio

English Language Learners in Literacy Workshops

Marsha Riddle Buly
Western Washington University

NCTE National Council of Teachers of English
1111 W. Kenyon Road, Urbana, Illinois 61801-1096

Staff Editor: Bonny Graham

Interior Design: Jenny Jensen Greenleaf

Cover Design: Pat Mayer

Cover Background Design: iStockphoto.com/aleksandarvelasevic

NCTE Stock Number: 22884

©2011 by the National Council of Teachers of English.

All rights reserved. No part of this publication may be reproduced or transmitted in any form or by any means, electronic or mechanical, including photocopy, or any information storage and retrieval system, without permission from the copyright holder. Printed in the United States of America.

It is the policy of NCTE in its journals and other publications to provide a forum for the open discussion of ideas concerning the content and the teaching of English and the language arts. Publicity accorded to any particular point of view does not imply endorsement by the Executive Committee, the Board of Directors, or the membership at large, except in announcements of policy, where such endorsement is clearly specified.

Every effort has been made to provide current URLs and email addresses, but because of the rapidly changing nature of the Web, some sites and addresses may no longer be accessible.

Library of Congress Cataloging-in-Publication Data

Riddle Buly, Marsha.
   English language learners in literacy workshops / Marsha Riddle Buly.
       p. cm.
   Includes bibliographical references.
   ISBN 978-0-8141-2288-4 (pbk)
   1. English language--Study and teaching--Foreign speakers.   I. Title.
   PE1128.A2E4873 2011
   428.2'4--dc23
                                                                2011035728

This book is dedicated to the two most amazing people in my life, my patient and encouraging husband Phil, and my less-patient yet incredibly motivating bilingual daughter, Halina Elizabeth. My world revolves around both of you.

Contents

Permission Acknowledgments

Page 28: Cultural relevance texts rubric reprinted with permission from *Academic Language for English Language Learners and Struggling Readers* by Yvonne S. Freeman and David E. Freeman. Copyright © 2009 by Yvonne S. Freeman and David E. Freeman. Published by Heinemann, Portsmouth, NH. All rights reserved.

Page 50: "10 Steps to Teaching and Learning Independence" adapted and reprinted with permission of Gail Boushey and Joan Moser.

Page 55: Acronym for ACTIVE thinking strategies developed by Barry Hoonan, middle school teacher, Bainbridge Island, Washington, based on *Mosaic of Thought* (Keene & Zimmerman, 1997).

Page 58: Figurative Language Rap reprinted courtesy of Rhythm, Rhyme, Results (http://www.educationalrap.com) and can be found at http://www.educationalrap.com/song/figurative-language.html.

Page 60: Common idioms in American English reprinted with permission of www.teacherjoe.us. See also www.teacherjoe.us/Idioms02.html.

Acknowledgments

Just as language learners need trusted peers with whom to read and share drafts, writers need trusted colleagues. I am thankful that I have more than one. The first is my amazing husband, a teacher who patiently reads, rereads, and reads yet again as I strive to organize my ideas into a more linear fashion. I also want to thank Tracy Coskie, who reads my work, knocks on my wall, and offers guidance without extinguishing my writing flame.

I have the opportunity to work with so many amazing teachers, some of whom you will meet in this book. In particular, I would like to thank Dawn Christiana, Michelle Hornof, Courtnie Mirabelli, Miguel Rivas, and Taraleen Rosen, who over the years have allowed me to keep my practice current by working with, observing, and discussing the language learners and literacy instruction in their mainstream classrooms, as well as the students themselves. Michelle and Jenna Harris also served as critical friends who read and offered insights into the early, quite rough, draft of this work.

Bonny Graham, the NCTE editor, is truly amazing. I want to thank her for supporting me as I wrote my first book.

I have the opportunity to work with many other thoughtful teachers and, through their trials and errors, as well as my own, to experience what works and what doesn't work for the growing numbers of bilingual learners in our wonderfully diverse schools.

Teachers rock.

Introduction

Our schools are increasingly diverse centers of multiple language learners. This trend will continue. In fact, demographers predict that within another seven years, up to 25 percent of students enrolled in elementary and secondary schools in the United States will have limited proficiency in English (Suárez-Orozco & Suárez-Orozco, 2003). In the best of worlds, with unlimited funds and highly qualified bilingual teachers in all languages, schools would capitalize on all language diversity, and we would have bilingual/biliteracy/bicultural programs with language-certified teachers teaching alongside mainstream classroom teachers in every classroom at every age level. There is overwhelming evidence of the benefits of bilingualism. For years, researchers have been finding cognitive and linguistic benefits for bilingual learners (August & Hakuta, 1998), in addition to the social and economic assets for all people that full academic bilingualism can bring (Miramontes, Nadeau, & Commins, 1997). And now we have evidence that early bilingualism can stave off Alzheimer's disease for up to four years (Bialystok, Craik, & Freedman, 2007). The implications of this latest finding alone on quality of life and diminished health care costs are compelling enough to make early bilingualism an educational priority for all residents of the United States, including those who speak only English at home.

The current reality, however, is that many of the growing numbers of bilingual students will spend all or part of their school day in general education or mainstream classrooms with teachers who do not speak their language. To further complicate instruction, at the same time that the number of language learners in classrooms is increasing, we continue to have many mainstream education teachers with little or no training in instructional understandings or strategies to engage and enhance the learning of language learners in mainstream classroom literacy instruction. The result is that we end up focusing on adding English, often disregarding the benefits of other languages students may bring when they enter our classrooms.

Even in the "perfect situation," teaching is hard work, but it doesn't have to be any harder with a roomful of diverse language learners. All of the students in our classrooms are diverse; all should expect to receive instruction that meets their individual needs. Regardless of our language of instruction, capitalizing on the benefits of biliteracy and multilingualism must remain a primary goal for students who come to us with a language other than English. Differentiated instruction based on the assessed needs and next steps of students is a key to success throughout any student's instructional journey. And while setting up and managing differentiated literacy instruction may seem too difficult or time-consuming for many teachers, literacy workshops provide just the answer in an easily manageable, accessible format.

This book is a result of my work with teachers and those becoming teachers. As I searched for the book I needed in my courses and workshops, I found many amazing books with helpful elements but no one single book that provided mainstream K–8 classroom teachers solid instructional ideas with a combined focus on reading, writing, and language workshops and on the diverse and growing numbers of language learners in the mainstream classroom. When I first sat down to draft a book, I planned to write about helping language learners by integrating literacy instruction and content areas in a workshop format. But each time I attempted to present this to teachers, I found that many didn't have experience working with language learners, or that their idea of a literacy workshop was very different from the successful workshop formats I had studied. Many models they shared with me didn't include the powerful explicit instruction possible within a workshop framework. So I needed to back up and begin with language learners in the literacy workshop from the perspective of the mainstream classroom teacher.

In the pages that follow, I have attempted to synthesize what I have learned, what I present, and what I have observed in classrooms with teachers who successfully reach their language learners. I draw on the material I use to teach future teachers and that I present to teachers in workshops. I have changed the names and details in the examples I use to illustrate practice, and many of my education colleagues may think an example is based on them; this is likely, but just as likely a specific example is based on a combination of several of the amazing educators I have had the opportunity to know. I have diligently attempted to give credit to the originators of ideas and quotes; however, I suspect I've missed some. I apologize in advance and ask that you let me know if I haven't acknowledged you or have given credit to the wrong educator. The creative and original work of educators deserves recognition.

I shared the first chapter with a newly certified teacher as she was working with seventh-grade classrooms comprising more than 50 percent English language learners, students at various levels of English acquisition. This teacher had both a K–8 and an ELL endorsement. After reading the chapter, she responded:

> I read the chapter and it is great! I find it very user friendly and it seems a tantalizing introduction to something I can't wait to read. I think it really synthesizes a lot

of great research and practices and puts them into a framework that is authentic and doable. I just need more experience in order to create mini-lessons I feel confident with.

That is what the remainder of the book will do for her and for you: provide support as you begin to develop or refine a workshop format with explicit instruction in reading, writing, and language *for all* the students in your classroom, language learners and native English speakers alike.

Chapter 1 provides a fundamental understanding of the rationale behind the literacy workshop format. Having this shared understanding is critical as we move into the chapters that follow. Chapter 1 includes a research-based framework for instruction as well as a framework for organizing the classroom. For many mainstream teachers, this is likely to be a refresher. For preservice teachers and novices to the workshop, it provides essential background information that will allow us to continue the journey through this book with a similar foundation of knowledge. The chapter ends with ideas for the teacher-reader to try, as well as recommendations for further reading from some of my favorite resources.

Chapter 2 explains why workshop approaches match what we know about effective research-based instructional structures for language learners. The chapter begins by presenting fundamental understandings with a focus on how cognitive demands and contextual support impact language learners (Cummins, 1994). I then describe alignments between components of the explicit literacy workshop format and the Sheltered Instruction Observation Protocol (SIOP) model (Echevarría, Vogt, & Short, 2008). Although this alignment is one of the unique aspects of the book, *English Language Learners in Literacy Workshops* is not designed to teach SIOP; it is designed to help mainstream teachers use literacy workshops to meet the differentiated needs of the language learners in their classrooms. Many excellent books cover the SIOP protocol, and the list at the end of Chapter 2 provides titles of just a few of the resources that focus exclusively on SIOP. My purpose for this chapter is to help teachers not familiar with valid theoretical work related to language learners, including SIOP, or for those unfamiliar with workshop formats, to understand how this research supports the literacy workshop as an effective instructional format for language learners.

Chapters 3, 4, and 5 focus on teacher instruction for each component of a literacy workshop, with an emphasis on the language learners in the classroom. Each chapter starts with a scenario from a classroom, followed by an explanation that includes instructional tips for a particular aspect of the literacy workshop. Each chapter ends with an immediate takeaway idea for the teacher-reader to try and suggestions for further reading.

In Chapter 6, I've collected and addressed common questions asked by practicing and future teachers. When appropriate, I have included suggestions for additional resources. I haven't listed every good question I've received, and I welcome your correspondence regarding additional questions related to language learners you may have as you read this book and other resources and as you implement or revise your literacy workshops. You can reach me at Marsha.RiddleBuly@wwu.edu.

My experience and my own reading preferences suggest that short, practical books have the most success with teachers and future teachers. This book does not answer all questions; it provides practical applications and answers for teachers, with recommendations for additional readings on different topics. I hope that what you read sparks your interest in further reading and study. Each chapter is designed to stand alone so that you can use the book in the way that best suits your instructional needs. That might mean starting with common questions or it might mean starting at the beginning and reading through. My hope is that you leave the book knowing more than you did when you started and with the hunger to continue the learning journey into the most effective literacy instruction for our diverse language learners.

Fundamentals of the
Literacy Workshop

If we want students to learn, we must show them how.

—STEPHANIE HARVEY, *NONFICTION MATTERS*

The literacy workshop is similar to *any* workshop. The word *workshop* itself suggests a group of people actively engaged in purposeful tasks. In this chapter, I explain my understanding of the fundamentals that provide the foundation of a workshop format. Like most terms used in education, *workshop* has been interpreted differently depending on the experience, theoretical base, and beliefs of the teacher (Robinson & Riddle Buly, 2007). To make sense of this book, we need to start with a shared beginning. For some of you, the following pages will be new information, which is why I provide an overview as well as suggest additional resources at the end of the chapter to further your understanding. For others, this chapter will provide both a review and a chance for me to clarify how I am interpreting the literacy workshop in the mainstream classroom. For still others, this chapter might offer the opportunity to view the literacy workshop from a perspective that differs from what you have experienced or considered in the past.

The foundational format of an effective, research-based workshop is basically the same regardless of the makeup of the students or of the subject taught. This first chapter focuses on the format of a workshop approach so that as you read further, you and I are on the same page when I discuss workshops and explicit mini-lessons. Subsequent chapters expand on this base to focus on language learners in the literacy workshop.

Students learn by "doing" in a workshop, with the guidance of a knowledgeable other. For the purposes of this book, this knowledgeable other is a teacher, although a knowledgeable other can be many things, among them a parent, an instructional assistant, another student, or a friend. A knowledgeable other is one who knows a bit more about a particular topic, skill, or idea and can support the learner because of that extra knowledge (Vygotsky, 1978). My high school experience as a pottery student illustrates this concept. I had the good fortune of a wonderful pottery teacher. When the pottery class began each day, Mr. Collins would gather all twenty-five of us around him, sophomores, juniors, and seniors, all with varying degrees of artistic skill or talent, and we would strain to see what he was doing. We all wanted to be in the front row watching this more knowledgeable other at work. Mr. Collins would model a skill, strategy, or technique that he was using with his clay and talk to us about it as he molded the clay. Once we had seen the technique, he often gave each of us a bit of clay so that we could try what he had just showed us, and we worked with the clay right there in front of him. Mr. Collins watched as we experimented, and if we needed more instruction, he would model again using his own clay or give us a specific suggestion based on what he saw us doing. Then he invited us to move to our own workspaces to continue working on our own creations. He suggested that we try for ourselves the techniques he had modeled if doing so made sense for the work we were doing that day.

When we started to work independently, Mr. Collins roved the room offering specific insights or instruction as we worked on our own pieces of clay. Some of us were more advanced than others, yet he found a way to move each of us forward with his suggestions and modeling. He also found a way to make sure that we all tried his suggestions. Some of us were working on pieces that could benefit from the technique he had modeled that day. Others of us couldn't incorporate the technique right away, but we knew it was something we would want to try in future projects. At the end of each class, Mr. Collins called us back together and we shared what we had tried or discovered related to the modeling he had done that day or on an earlier day.

The workshop format relies on this understanding of a gradual release of responsibility combined with very short, focused, and explicit instruction based on ongoing formative assessment of student strengths and needs. Some teachers find the format so effective that they use the same framework for social studies, science, and math. The framework is the same regardless of the area of instruction or the makeup of the students. Powerful workshops require a gradual supported release of responsibility from teacher to student, an instructional focus on the specific needs of a particular group of students, and an authentic reason for the instruction.

Gradual Release of Responsibility: The Apprenticeship

The instructional components that frame the idea of gradual release are shared in design, yet distinctly labeled, by educational experts in special education, English language development, and general education. There are many iterations of the same basic idea. The first illustration and language probably originated with Pearson and Gallagher's (1983) work at the Center for the Study of Reading, but it has been adapted and revised by many, including Lucy Calkins (1994; Calkins et al., 2003, 2006; Calkins, Tolan, Ehrenworth, Khan, & Mooney, 2010), Margaret Mooney (1990), Irene Fountas and Gay Su Pinnell (1996, 2001), and more recently by Douglas Fisher and his colleagues (Fisher, Rothenberg, & Frey, 2007). Figure 1.1 is a variation on one of the common illustrations of gradual release of responsibility.

The reading, writing, or language workshop works in the same way. The teacher provides a brief and explicit lesson about a skill, strategy, or technique related to reading, writing, or language. The teacher explains what it is, why it's important, and when it's useful. Then the teacher shows the students how the teacher, as a more knowledgeable other, employs the strategy, skill, or technique. Together with the teacher, the students then try what has been taught. The teacher carefully observes and provides further examples or explanations if needed. Students then have an opportunity to independently try what has been taught while the teacher guides or instructs individuals or small groups of students. At the end of the workshop, students gather together with the teacher to share what they have learned or tried related to the teacher's mini-lesson.

This doesn't mean that all students will use what was taught that day, or even in the near future, in their independent work. It means that most have demonstrated a basic understanding of what was taught and that they will feel encouraged to try or use the skill or strategy when it is appropriate in their independent work. The strategy or skill introduced is one that the teacher believes many students are ready for in their current work, so many—but not all—will immediately apply the teaching point in their independent work. Some teachers of K–2 students do always expect

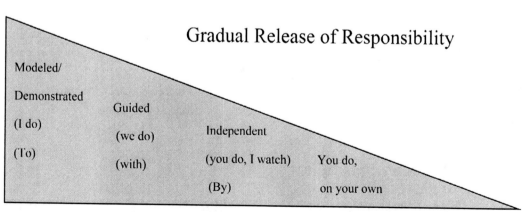

FIGURE 1.1: The gradual release of responsibility model.

the students to try what is modeled right away, finding that the students struggle to remember it later if they don't apply it immediately. Teachers of older students can also expect all students to briefly try what was modeled before they return to their work of the day, as we did in my high school pottery class.

When students are working independently, the teacher continues to monitor, support, guide, and reinforce the teaching point in small groups or one-on-one with individual students. If he or she sees a common need across many students, the teacher takes a step back to provide additional whole-group instruction. If only a few students demonstrate a need, the teacher may reteach and provide additional demonstration, modeling, and explanation to just one person or to a small group. The ultimate goal is for our students to use what was taught in other situations, completely on their own.

An easy way to remember how this gradual release of responsibility apprenticeship frames instruction in the workshop is to break the learning into components. From the teacher's perspective, there are four components: I do, we do, you do, and you do *over time*. "I do" constitutes teacher modeling, "we do" is guided or shared practice, "you do" is independent practice with teacher watching, and "you do over time" is students independently choosing and accurately using the strategy, skill, technique, or procedure. Following are more detailed descriptions of each of these critical areas of instruction in the literacy workshop.

The first step is demonstration or modeling in the form of an explicit lesson, when students watch and listen (Margaret Mooney calls this "read to"; it's part of the "connect" and "teach" components described by Lucy Calkins; and others call it "I do").

Guided practice is when students try the strategies, skills, or procedures with the guidance of the teacher (Margaret Mooney calls this "read with"; it's part of the "engage" component described by Lucy Calkins; and others call it "we do").

Independent practice occurs when students have time to practice the strategies and skills they are learning and those they already know (Margaret Mooney calls this "read by"; it's what is suggested in the "link" described by Lucy Calkins; and others call it "you do").

And "you do on your own" is the final outcome of instruction, when the learner owns the strategy, skill, procedure, or technique and is using it accurately in other situations.

When gradual release of responsibility is used to frame explicit teaching points in a literacy workshop, the result is powerful instruction and learning.

Knowing What to Teach

On the first day of teaching my first class of eager kindergarten students, I learned one of my most important lessons as a teacher, a lesson affirmed with every subsequent group of students from any grade level I have ever taught: just because students are in the same grade does not mean they are ready for the same instruction, and just because they speak a common home language doesn't mean they have the same level of literacy in their home language or in the language of school. I quickly found that trying to follow a set curriculum for all students did not work. The curriculum was appropriate for some, too easy for others, too difficult for several, and not the best teaching approach for many. This was further affirmed during teacher–parent conferences when parents would tell me that the grade-level instruction was too easy (or too hard) for their son or daughter, followed by the dreaded question of how I planned to meet the specific needs of their son or daughter. Any parent who has tried to rush a toddler to stand, walk, talk, or move away from diapers knows that children vary in what, when, and how they learn to do things. Some require different methods to get going. In my experience, what works with child one rarely works with child two or three the same way in the same home. The students who come to our PreK–12 classrooms vary in what they can and will do and what they are ready to learn from the day they are born (and even earlier as they are developing). We need high expectations for all students, the same standards we have for the most proficient students in the class. But how and when students meet our goals will differ. They will walk at different times, talk at different times, learn a language or languages differently, grasp reading, writing, and language at different times and in different ways. They will need instruction and opportunities based on their individual assessed needs, and those assessments must consider the language understandings of each student.

For the general classroom teacher with twenty to thirty-five students, this means that the individual strengths and needs of each student in any group must drive instructional decisions. The dilemma comes in trying to find a manageable classroom format that allows teachers to meet and work with individuals, small groups, and the whole class based on those varying instructional strengths and needs. The format of the workshop provides just such a structure for classroom teachers. Within this structure are opportunities for teachers to spend quality time with students through explicit, focused, and short lessons matched to the needs of a large group, small groups, or individuals. State standards and district expectations may provide a teacher's overarching goals, but the needs of the students determine where in the standards or materials that teacher will focus, with the expectation that all students meet standards as soon as they are able.

Michelle Hornof, a fifth-grade teacher, plans for the year before she even meets her students. She uses her experience, state standards, and district expectations as guides as she develops her curricular plans. However, Michelle's plans are not rigid. She adjusts as needed as the year goes by. Curriculum planning is similar to planning a trip. Before you start, you know your destination. You also know key places you might visit along the way. But your route might vary from your original plan as you

move toward the destination; you might stay longer at one attraction than you had anticipated, or you might experience car problems that require attention before you move on. For example, Michelle knows she will be teaching a unit on writing poetry in the spring. She also knows she will teach strategies for reading nonfiction in January. The specifics of what she will teach and how she will teach these units will be based on the needs of her students as the time draws near. But she knows the destination. Michelle learned this way of thinking about instruction from Lucy Calkins's (1994) *The Art of Teaching Writing*.

Likewise, when Marta, a new bilingual learner in my third-grade class, arrives with vocabulary needs that the other students don't have, I can focus specific one-on-one or small-group lessons during independent reading at her instructional level. At the same time, I can structure appropriate one-on-one or small-group teaching points for Samuel, who is reading materials usually read by fifth graders. By focusing on the needs of the students, I purposefully differentiate instruction and meet each student at his or her "zone of proximal development" (Vygotsky, 1978) or instructional level (Clay, 1993). Stephen Krashen (1981, 1982, 1994), well-known for his theories on language acquisition, suggests that we consider "comprehensible input + 1" when thinking about the bilingual learners in our classrooms, a concept that fits with how we need to think about *all* learners. *Comprehensible input + 1* is very similar to *instructional level*, often referred to by reading teachers and other educators, as well as the *zone of proximal development* (ZPD) attributed to Lev Vygotsky (1978), terms likely to be familiar to most mainstream classroom teachers. "Comprehensible input" means that material is presented in a way we can understand independently. For example, books that are at our independent reading level are comprehensible. When we add the "+ 1," we have moved to the *instructional level*, the level at which we are ready to understand with assistance from a knowledgeable other.

The concept behind comprehensible input + 1 is analogous to the situation of the protagonist in "Goldilocks and the Three Bears." Goldilocks tries the bears' porridge and finds that one bowl is too hot, one too cold, and one just right. She also tries the chairs and the beds—one is too hard, one is too soft, and one is just right. The same occurs in our instruction. We might teach a lesson that is too hard, or frustrating, for a student, because the student is not yet ready for the instruction. We can teach a lesson that is too easy, or at an independent level, which does little to move the student forward in his or her learning. Or we can teach a student a lesson that is "just right," or at the instructional level (comprehensible input + 1), of that student for the particular strategy, skill, or content being taught. This should be our goal as teachers, to teach all learners at their individual instructional levels in a manner that makes the material comprehensible for each learner.

Purposeful Learning: Knowing the "Why"

The well-known author of the Harry Potter series, J. K. Rowling, seems to understand children and the too-frequent disconnect between what happens within the walls of our schools and what happens in the "real world." A wonderful example of this is demonstrated when Professor Umbridge says to Harry Potter, "This is school, Mr. Potter, not the real world" (Rowling, 2003, p. 244). This statement articulates what many students feel about their experiences in our classrooms; there doesn't seem to be a clear connection between academic content and their real worlds, now or in the future. Students need a purpose that makes sense to them, provides a link to something meaningful, or is authentic. Nell Duke and her colleagues explain authentic literacy activities as those that replicate or are closely related to the same types of literacy activities that occur in people's day-to-day lives (Duke, Purcell-Gates, Hall, & Tower, 2006). We do not learn to read or write simply to read or write; we learn to read or write to effectively navigate the world, to learn new information, to share information and ideas. Clearly, when students see a purpose that goes beyond the walls of the classroom, there is a greater chance of engagement, learning, and application.

Tracy Coskie (2009) identifies three purposes for writing, which she labels real-world writing, real audiences, and real connections, to illustrate how adults use literacy for authentic purposes. An example of real-world writing is a sign that helps her to be careful in a bird habitat, because caring for the environment is so important in her life. As an example of real audiences, she listed the exhibit guides her husband was asked to write for a local museum's historical motorcycle exhibition. And for an example of real connections, Coskie shared her friend's recently discovered passion for blogging with other fantasy football players. Our students need the same types of authentic purposes for what they are learning in school. They need to see how what we are teaching relates to life outside the four walls of the classroom.

This doesn't mean that an authentic audience can't be found within the walls of the school. In her bilingual fourth-grade classroom, Mrs. Rosen wanted to set a purpose for researching biospheres by providing her students with an authentic audience. Coincidentally, the second-grade students had just finished reading *The A, B, C of the Biosphere* (Imagine a Biosphere Series) by Max Finch and Mary Beath (1993). The students were really interested in the topic. As the second- and fourth-grade teachers talked, an authentic audience and purpose materialized that would encourage the fourth graders to dig deeper into the subject of biospheres. The diverse-language fourth-grade students would research and present what they learned about a topic of interest to their equally diverse second-grade language-learning buddies.

Mrs. Rosen started by bringing in numerous picture books about biospheres that both the second- and fourth-grade students read and discussed. As a result, they identified specific questions of interest to students in both grade levels. Small groups of fourth graders selected a question to research. The expectation was that the student groups would research a question and then share what they found in an interesting manner with their second-grade buddies. The students did not have choice in topic; everyone was researching biospheres. They did have a choice of genre in which to prepare and share their findings. By providing the students with a purpose and choice, Mrs. Rosen motivated the students to locate, dig into, and read from different sources. They were engaged in planning and writing about what they had learned, and they were excited about sharing what they learned with others. While they were research-ing, Mrs. Rosen taught specific, explicit lessons on reading, writing, and language immediately applicable to the authentic reading, writing, and language in which the fourth graders were engaged. She also taught small groups specific lessons related to the genre or presentation each group had chosen to share their findings. The students derived meaning from this study because they had an authentic audience of younger students who they cared about and who were interested in the information they would be sharing. To effectively share that information, they happily worked on their reading, writing, and language skills. Some groups chose to write plays, some created experiments and shared the results, some wrote picture books, while others created brochures. All engaged in the process of learning and writing about science.

In Michelle Hornof's fifth-grade language arts classroom, the students were look-ing forward to the annual overnight trip to study the environment at Mountain School. As so often in schools, the trip would not take place unless the students raised funds. The students worked on writing persuasive letters to an audience of their choice, combining a real-world audience with a real-world purpose. All were asking for a donation to attend Mountain School, an end-of-the-year activity. The fifth graders were expected to use a letter format, write a persuasive letter, and address an envelope. However, students could choose to whom they would write the letter (audience), as long as the recipient was authentic. The students sent the letters at the end of the unit. (The process of this letter writing unit is described in detail in Chapter 4.)

I invite you to take a moment to think back to your own years as a student, in any grade, and the times you were told to do something or try something simply because the teacher requested that you do so. My response, as a child and as an adult, is "Why should I do this? Who cares?" That is the same response our students often have in our classrooms—often internally, sometimes aloud. In addition to needing to know the steps involved in how to do something, it's human nature to want to know *why* we are being asked to do something, and why or how it connects to the rest of our lives. These connections are what make certain activities worth doing. When we understand the reason for doing something, we are much more likely to be interested in learning and to internalize the learning.

Scott Paris and his colleagues (Paris, Wixson, & Palincsar, 1986) suggest that part of a teacher's job is to clearly explain strategies so that students can see the purpose and sense behind them. In this book, I use the term *strategies* to represent those things we have taught students that we hope they will internalize, practice, and use on their own in new situations. Having strategies is the mark of a skilled reader or writer. Take driving a car. If I am a skilled driver, I drive almost automatically, without having to think too much about what I'm doing. But if I encounter a problem while I'm driving, like a big patch of ice, I become very conscious of the situation and need to rely on the defensive driving strategies I've learned to help me navigate the danger. If I'm lucky, I have a big tool box of strategies that I've been taught and perhaps practiced for just such a time: encountering ice in real life. I have internalized these strategies so that they come to me almost automatically when I encounter ice. I might swerve around the ice, I might tap my brakes, or I might drive through the ice with no brakes. The strategy I use will depend on the situation, on how dangerous I perceive the ice to be, whether there are cars close to me, whether there is room to swerve, and whether I have time to consider options. But I have several strategies I can access to assist me in this situation. If one doesn't work, I might have time to try a different one. This is how I use the term *strategy* throughout this book—as teachers, we want our students to have options that will help them successfully navigate both familiar and new situations. Although Paris and his colleagues wrote specifically about reading strategies, their ideas hold true for any strategy or procedure we or our students are learning. When we know why we are doing something, how it will help us, and when to use it, we are likely to be more receptive to learning how to do it, as well as more likely to apply and continue to use what we have been taught in new situations.

Understanding why something is being taught is important for all of us, but probably even more important for bilingual learners. In their book *"Reading Don't Fix No Chevys": Literacy in the Lives of Young Men*, Michael Smith and Jeffrey Wilhelm (2002), both former high school teachers, share their learning about how boys in secondary classrooms often disengage with school literacy. They found that although many students read materials outside of the classroom that feel relevant to their lives *that day*, those same students see little relevance to the reading they're asked to do within the four walls of the classroom. Although these students understand that school is a stepping stone to success, that reason isn't immediately relevant enough to ensure their active participation in academic reading. They need relevance to the present. Elizabeth Moje has also written extensively about the critical role of engagement in literacy, especially for adolescents. For example, Moje (2006) describes a student identified academically as a struggling reader who worked very hard outside of the classroom to make sense of directions for a video game. Much to the teacher's amazement, when this student had an immediate and personal purpose for reading, he worked hard at it. The lesson for teachers is that our students need an out-of-classroom reason for doing what we ask them to do, or at the very least, a purpose that is meaningful to them. For small children, doing something "for the teacher" might be enough motivation to get them started, but imagine how much more we've added to their learning if students have an authentic reason that goes beyond the classroom. And if we can't think of an authentic reason or purpose for what we're teaching, perhaps we should be teaching something else.

The Workshop

The individual components of the workshop are similar regardless of the students in your classroom, the content of instruction, or the length of time of the workshop. The differences or changes will be in your teaching points. Lucy Calkins and her colleagues have expanded the components of the workshop to include seven distinct elements that many find helpful in planning for instruction. A clear description can be found in the Units of Study materials that Calkins and her colleagues (2003, 2006; Calkins, Tolan, Ehrenworth, Khan, & Mooney, 2010) have published in recent years. Table 1.1 draws from this work.

We know that the most successful teachers spend the majority of their time providing instruction rather than giving directions (Taylor, Pressley, & Pearson, 2000). Yet Dolores Durkin's (1978–1979) seminal work illustrated how much time teachers spent—and many still spend—giving instructions rather than actually instructing (or teaching). The lesson format in well-run literacy workshops allows for direct and explicit instruction, the kind of instruction that has been shown to improve reading comprehension for low-achieving readers (Dole, 2000). *Explicitness* means being clear about a teaching point—not assuming that students already know what we are teaching, not leaving them to guess, but also not teaching them something they already know. The explicit lesson focus usually occurs within the first ten minutes of the workshop and is the key to success.

In the following description of a mini-lesson, I provide an *ideal* time frame for each section. When I participated in the training for Guided Language Acquisition Design (GLAD), we were taught a strategy the trainers called "10 and 2" (Brechtal,

Component	Teacher is . . .	Students are . . .
1. Connect/Purpose (What, Why, When) (1–2 minutes)	Providing a purpose for the teaching point with a link to previous learning	Listening and connecting
2. Model/Provide Information (How) (3–5 minutes)	Demonstrating or showing students *how* to use the strategy, skill, technique, or procedure	Listening and learning
3. Guided Practice (2–3 minutes)	Observing and guiding	Trying the skill, strategy, or procedure in front of the teacher
4. Link to Independent Work (1–2 minutes)	Connecting what was taught to students' work and setting	Considering how they will use what they have been taught
5. Independent Work (30–60 minutes)	Conferring, teaching, monitoring, observing, assessing, identifying students to share	Engaged in their work
6. Sharing (2–4 minutes)	Directing, facilitating	Sharing what they've done related to the day's lesson
7. Close (1–2 minutes)	Restating, linking to future work	Listening, connecting

TABLE 1.1: Components of the Literacy Workshop

2001). The basic idea is that most people can focus for no more than ten minutes at a time, so for every ten minutes of input learners need two minutes for reflection or processing of the information. And for kindergarten or younger students, the time is probably more like 5-and-1. In my experience with students of many ages, including adults, 10-and-2 is a guide that works most of the time. When I'm modeling, demonstrating, or talking, I try to check the clock when I start and ensure that I pause at around ten minutes for two minutes (or more) of processing before I provide more information or instructions. If I don't observe this time frame, I see my students' attention drifting away. At times, your explicit lessons might, and probably will, take longer for different parts of the lesson, but aiming for the ideal and observing the 10-and-2 rule will help the lesson be explicit, focused, and thus more likely keep your students' attention.

Connect/Purpose (What, Why, When) (I do)
(1–2 minutes)

The connect/purpose piece of the workshop is a time for you to explicitly and concisely provide a purpose for the teaching point with a link to previous learning. But the purpose needs to go beyond this link to a previous lesson. Including a real-life purpose that extends past the classroom walls is powerful for engaging learning. The connect portion is short, only one to two minutes. Within this brief time, you must *explicitly tell* students WHAT the strategy is, WHY it is important or useful, and WHEN the strategy, skill, or procedure is used. Gerald Duffy and his colleagues (Duffy, Roehler, Meloth, Vavrus, Book, Putnam, & Wesselman, 1986) call this declarative and conditional knowledge. Lucy Calkins would ask us to notice that the teacher does the telling at this point. To keep it quick and clear, we avoid asking students, "Remember when we . . . ? Why did we do that?" These are the kinds of questions that eat up time and don't necessarily end in the answers you seek. Rather than lose precious instructional attention time, remind students what was taught, what will be learned, why it is important, and when it is useful: "Yesterday we . . . Today we are going to . . . because . . ."

Model/Provide Information (How) (I do)
(3–5 minutes)
Modeling or providing information during a mini-lesson is when you demonstrate to students *how* they can use the strategy, skill, technique, or procedure. Gerald Duffy and colleagues (1986) refer to this as procedural knowledge. The goal of this part of the lesson is for the students to understand the steps—the procedural knowledge—of what is being taught. Janice Almasi (2003) wrote about strategic instruction, finding that among declarative, conditional, and procedural knowledge, it is procedural knowledge that more teachers skip. Rather than instruct through modeling, demonstration, or think-aloud, the teachers she observed explained an activity or gave instructions, similar to what Durkin (1978–1979) found. Explaining an activity or giving instruction is not the same as teaching or showing students how to do something.

To demonstrate, you can use think-alouds or talk-throughs. Both allow you to make your thinking public, thinking aloud about what you are teaching as you demonstrate. For example, if the teaching point is inferring, you might show the students how you infer by explaining what is happening in your head. Rather than simply saying something like, "I just made an inference" and continuing to read, you can think aloud about how you made the inference, explicitly sharing and describing your thoughts, what connections you're making, and what information your inference is based on. So, for example, if you're reading *Clementine* (Pennypacker,

2006), you might say something like, *As I read this paragraph, and I think about what has happened so far, what I know from my own life, and what we already know about Clementine, I am inferring. My thinking is leading me to infer that Clementine is going to get in big trouble for cutting Margaret's hair*. Then you continue to read until the next point that allows you to explicitly model an inference, again thinking aloud or talking through how you came to that conclusion.

Guided Practice (we do)

(2–3 minutes)

The purpose of guided practice is to give students an opportunity to try out the skill, strategy, or procedure you've demonstrated while still under your observant eye. Guided practice with partners or small groups is especially powerful for language learners because it gives them the chance to talk together, which helps them clarify understandings. This is also the time to informally assess their progress and decide whether students are ready to move on to independent practice or whether to take a step back, provide more support, and reteach or expand on your teaching. If assessment suggests reteaching would be helpful, you might decide to stop for the day and return to the lesson another time. Or you might have additional examples or models ready and can provide those at this time. Often you will notice that many students seem to "get it" and that just a few need more support before moving on to independent work. In this case, you might meet with that small group while other students are engaged in independent practice.

Link to Independent Work/Engage

(1–2 minutes)

If most of the students seem ready to move on to independent work, spend a few moments to help them see how to use the skill or strategy independently and set expectations for them. It is critical that you convey to the students that if what you've taught fits their work today, they should go ahead and try it on their own. If it doesn't, you don't expect them to try the newly taught strategy or skill today, but instead to practice it on their own when doing so makes sense for their work. If you expect every student to need the strategy or skill eventually, you might set a date in the future, saying something like, *Today is the 1st of February; by February 15 I think you will all have had an opportunity to use what I taught today. Please sign up for a conference when what I just taught makes sense to try in your work*. You can then track who has used this strategy and who might still need additional assistance. Your expectation might be that during independent work, students will try the strategy and be ready to report out during share time, or that they might explain why a strategy introduced wasn't pertinent to their work for the day.

Independent Work Time (you do)
(30–60 minutes)
Independent work time allows you to differentiate instruction. You can confer with students, reinforce teaching points with individuals or small groups, or introduce new teaching points. I elaborate on independent work time in the following section.

Sharing (at the end of the workshop)
(2–4 minutes)
Near the end of the workshop, pull students back together for a time to share, focusing on the teaching point of the lesson. Often you will have asked a few students during conferencing to individually share what each noticed or tried related to the teaching point. These are usually students you have had a conference with, not just any student raising a hand. This is a time for students to share different ways they have used what was taught, including struggles as well as successes they may have had. As students share, engage them in metacognitive thinking about the strategies, helping all students recognize that their individual backgrounds will vary their learning experiences and that there can be more than one successful strategy for any particular situation.

Close
(1–2 minutes)
The workshop ends with you briefly but very clearly restating the teaching point in student-friendly language, including *what* it is, *why* it's important, and *when* it's useful. This is the time to get students enthusiastic about continuing the work they've done today or trying what others have shared. It's also a time for students to start making plans for the next workshop.

Figure 1.2 illustrates how many teachers divide up the time provided for literacy workshop, regardless of the length of the workshop (e.g., 45 or 60 or 90 minutes).

Back to Independent Work Time

Nestled within the components of the workshop is a large chunk of time for independent work. Having students independently engaged in meaningful reading, writing, or language work is what allows you to provide differentiated instruction and assessment.

How you structure this time will vary depending on the needs of the students and your comfort level with students working on their own, but it is the heart of the workshop. Having this time to engage in the work on their own is critical for students to develop as readers, writers, and language users. Having this time is also essential for you, allowing you to meet with individuals or flexible groups to reinforce, teach, and assess.

Key point 1: You will be even more active once independent work begins. You have multiple options to choose from for engaging students. You might, for example, teach individuals or small groups of students who need more support on the teaching point, roam the room and conference with individuals, assess student understanding, or teach small guided groups of students who have other specific needs or who are ready for a new teaching point.

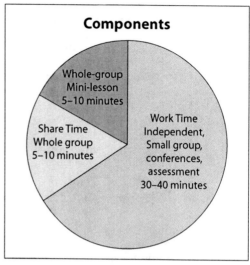

FIGURE 1.2: Components of the literacy workshop.

Key point 2: Establish a system by which students can let you know if they need you. I like to keep a list on the whiteboard (modeled in a mini-lesson) where students write their names if they need me. I let the students know that I will check in with them between teaching moments, but they are not to interrupt another student's learning opportunity. Knowing how to get the teacher's attention is especially important for English language learners. If they are confused about anything, they can add their name to the whiteboard, drawing my attention. Quite often, by the time I move to students on the list, most will have figured out a way to solve whatever it was they needed.

Key point 3: Stay mobile. Rather than calling the students to you, move to the students yourself. This provides two critical outcomes: (1) students around those who are receiving instruction can listen in on an instructional conversation; again, this is particularly helpful for bilingual learners because it is often beneficial to hear something explained

20 minutes	*Individual conferences* allow the teacher to meet with three to five individuals as the students settle into their work and to manage the classroom through quiet reminders or check-ins as the teacher walks from one student to another.
10 minutes	*Small-group work* allows the teacher to work with one small group while other students are engaged in independent or partner work.
5 minutes	*Transition and check in* with individuals as needed.
10 minutes	*Small-group work* allows the teacher to work with a second small group while other students are engaged in independent or partner work.

TABLE 1.2: Example of a 45-Minute Independent Work Schedule

in more than one way, and (2) you have an opportunity to quickly check in with language learners so that if someone is confused, practice time isn't wasted.

Table 1.2 provides an example of how one third-grade teacher breaks up independent work time in her classroom. The length of independent work time will vary depending on the students' levels of independence and how long you have for the workshop as a whole. In a 60-minute workshop, the goal time would be 30–40 minutes for independent work. In a 90-minute reading block, the goal might be two 30-minute blocks of independent time, with a mini-lesson in the middle to refocus students.

Records of Learning

Throughout the school day, it is important to takes notes, for which you'll need to maintain an observational note-taking system, a way to keep notes about what you are learning about the students in relation to specific instruction. I call these Records of Learning. I keep a separate "Record of Learning" spiral notebook for each subject, and in each notebook I write each student's name on a separate page. I write my observational notes, list any teaching points that we discuss, list next steps, and include a date. Figure 1.3 is an example from my Reading Record of Learning for Luna, a third-grade language learner. The note system is my own; you will undoubtedly work out your own system as you experiment with different ways to keep notes that make sense for you. These Records of Learning become the primary tool I use when planning upcoming units of study and teaching points. If I have kept clear records, I need only consult my spiral notebooks as I plan for whole-group, small-group, and individual teaching. I also use these Records of Learning for teacher–parent conferences and as a data source for report cards or progress reports.

Luna

Notes/Observations	Teaching Pts / Next Steps
9/16 Picking books during IR—changing books frequently	How to pick a book —interests topics
9/12 ML – Pick a book Pg 27 ORR – ✓✓ flé/s← flipping	Stamina ←Reinforce
9/20 ML – Pick a book series	Prediction
9/30 series Book – Junie B CLR Predicting / Text/Text + Text) me	Reinforce ML Predict / infer
10/05 Tlkng during IR – –Has finished Junie B – discuss/read a bit Weird school Days –	Pcking books / mvng on

FIGURE 1.3: A Reading Record of Learning for Luna, a third-grade language learner.

Summary

In this chapter, I have illustrated the following points. A workshop is:

1. *A framework for organizing instruction.* The workshop is not a curriculum, nor is it a set of specific materials. The workshop includes explicit instruction that is short, purposeful, and follows a familiar structure. Teachers strive to keep

concise lessons to about 10 minutes and focused on one teaching point at a time.

2. *An apprenticeship model.* A more knowledgeable other, usually the teacher but sometimes an instructional assistant, a parent, or even another student, models the strategy, skill, or procedure that others will learn. The students then try this strategy, skill, or procedure themselves in a nonthreatening environment, with guidance and a gradual release of responsibility from the more knowledgeable other.

3. *An instructional time when the needs of the students drive the teacher's lessons.* Curriculum, standards, materials, and scopes and sequences are resources in a workshop, and the teacher decides what needs to be taught. Those decisions are focused on the standards and based on students' needs, which determine necessary next steps in their learning while also providing the critical time for teachers to differentiate instruction through conferences or work with small groups of students.

4. *An instructional time when students understand the purpose of what they are doing, and that purpose goes beyond "for the teacher."* Whenever possible and applicable, students can identify a meaningful purpose for workshop activity that extends beyond the walls of the classroom.

5. *The critical time of the instructional day in which students need to independently engage in reading, writing, or language work.* An extended independent work time provides students the essential time to practice and grow as readers, writers, and language users.

A Time to Try . . .

1. Think about the time you currently devote to reading instruction. Which of the elements of the workshop are you already including in your instruction? Are there other elements you could add immediately?

2. Think of a specific skill or strategy your class is struggling with (e.g., lining up, getting a drink of water, sharpening a pencil). Try writing an explicit mini-lesson using the format that provides a purpose for this skill and allows for the gradual release of responsibility to your students. The more you plan your lessons this way, the easier they become!

Some Favorite Resources

Calkins, L., et al. (2003). *Units of study for primary writing: A yearlong curriculum.* Portsmouth, NH: FirstHand.

Calkins, L., et al. (2006). *Units of study for teaching writing: Grades 3–5.* Portsmouth, NH: FirstHand.

Calkins, L., Tolan, K., Ehrenworth, M., Khan, H. A., & Mooney, J. (2010). *Units of study for teaching reading, grades 3–5: A curriculum for the reading workshop.* Portsmouth, NH: Heinemann.

Coskie, T. L. (2009). Building in authenticity. *School Talk, 14*(3), 1–2.

Ellis, L., & Marsh, J. (2007). *Getting started: The reading-writing workshop, grades 4–8.* Portsmouth, NH: Heinemann.

Fletcher, R., & Portalupi, J. (2001). *Writing workshop: The essential guide.* Portsmouth, NH: Heinemann.

Fountas, I. C., & Pinnell, G. S. (2001). *Guiding readers and writers grades 3–6: Teaching comprehension, genre, and content literacy.* Portsmouth, NH: Heinemann.

Mooney, M. E. (1990). *Reading to, with, and by children.* Katonah, NY: Richard C. Owen.

2

Language Learners in the Literacy Workshop

Човекът е толкова пъти човек, колкото езика знае
(Čovekăt e tolkova păti čovek, kolkoto ezika znae)

The more languages you know, the more you are a person.

—BULGARIAN SAYING

I began my educational career thirty years ago as a first- and second-grade combination classroom teacher in Southern California. My students were a diverse group of bilingual learners, and I was a monolingual English-speaking teacher with no formal training in meeting the unique needs of English language learners. I hadn't had experiences or even studied methods to meet the needs of the diverse language learners in my classroom, such as explicit instruction or sheltered learning, and my colleagues didn't seem to know any more than I did. I didn't know where to start. The language learners in my classroom were often extremely quiet, and when I asked if they understood something, they would nod as if saying "yes." I didn't realize that nodding did not mean they understood. I knew almost nothing about the acquisition of language or how to support language learning.

As a first-year teacher, I thought I should know everything, so I kept my insecurities private. I didn't want to be discovered. Fast-forward thirty years. My experiences suggest that many mainstream classroom teachers still lack experience and training in how to effectively work with language learners. Fortunately for the growing number of bilingual learners in our schools, educators and teacher educators know much more than we did when I entered the field. Just as students negotiate meaning, take risks, and try different strategies to increase their understanding, we as teachers need to negotiate meaning, take risks, and ask questions of our colleagues in the field to improve our own instruction.

In this chapter, I share what I've come to understand about effective, research-based instructional protocols for language learning and how implementation suits the framework of the literacy workshop. Equally important, I share what I've learned about contexts for learning and cognitive demand, including the importance of culturally relevant instruction and truly knowing students. I include some ways that you can get to know your students as well as ways you can help them feel more at ease in your classroom. I end the chapter with an example and explanation of simple considerations that will enhance the literacy workshop for your language learners.

Theory

When I began to learn about language learners in the late 1980s, I studied the theories of Jim Cummins (1979, 1981, 1994) and Stephen Krashen (1981, 1982, 1994), among others. Cummins's and Krashen's work was fundamental in laying the foundation for my further learning. From Cummins I learned that there was a difference between conversational and academic language and that the language learners who could easily converse with me about their weekend might not understand the materials I was attempting to teach. Krashen compelled me to think about the context in which I was trying to instruct and how important students' self-confidence is for language learning (1981). But I wasn't adequately considering the crucial role that my students' backgrounds, language, and knowledge—all of their previous life experiences—played in their language acquisition. I was considering only one side of the child, the side I could easily see.

Content Considerations

Jim Cummins's early work (1979) on linguistic theories provided educators with an opportunity to explore basic interpersonal communicative skills (BICS) and cognitive academic language proficiency (CALP). Originally, he described these terms as the difference between social language and academic language, or conversational and educational language, specifically in reference to language learners in educational settings. The terms helped many educators, myself included, begin to understand how important knowing how students acquire language is for our instruction. Although the original acronyms of BICS and CALP are still often used by educators, Cummins has since elaborated on the differences between conversational and academic language to include the social and educational environment in which an event occurs. Basically, how complicated something is to learn depends on how much attention a learner has to put toward the learning. If the language is difficult and the learner must focus hard on the language itself, there may be little attention left over to put toward learning the concepts that language describes. If the concept, or cognitive demand, is difficult for the learner but the language and the environment for learning it are supportive, the learner has greater ability to focus on the concept to be learned.

To help us understand how this difference factors into our instruction, Cummins used a quadrant pictorial to show the intersection of social and educational demands with language. Drawing from Jim Cummins's (1994) and Pauline Gibbons's (2002) work, Trish Skillman, director of Teaching English to Speakers of Other Languages (TESOL), added examples to demonstrate different events in language learners' academic lives and where they might fall on the intersection of cognitive and contextual demands (see Figure 2.1). For example, a conversation between two students at recess about how to use playground equipment is highly context embedded—they are on the playground, next to the object of discussion—and cognitively does not demand much of them because the language is conversational, the students are able to clarify with each other, and they have visual support from the equipment on the playground. This interaction would fall in quadrant A of Figure 2.1. However, a teacher talking in front of a classroom about an unfamiliar topic with few or no pictures and no actual models is providing instruction that is both context reduced and cognitively demanding, so the interaction will be more difficult for language learners to understand—the language is new and the concept is new. This interaction would fall in quadrant D, where learning will be extremely difficult. Gibbons (1991), another language educator and a former student of Cummins, uses the terms *playground language* and *classroom language* when describing the intersection of cognitive demand and context differences:

> This playground language includes the language which enables children to make friends, join in games and take part in a variety of day-to-day activities that develop and maintain social contacts. It usually occurs in face-to-face contact, and is thus highly dependent on the physical and visual context, and on gesture and body language. Fluency with this kind of language is an important part of language development; without it a child is isolated from the normal social life of the playground. . . .
>
> But playground language is very different from the language that teachers use in the classroom, and from the language that we expect children to learn to use. The language of the playground is not the language associated with learning in mathematics, or social studies, or science. The playground situation does not normally offer children the opportunity to use such language as: *if we increase the angle by 5 degrees, we could cut the circumference into equal parts*. Nor does it normally require the language associated with the higher order thinking skills, such as hypothesizing, evaluating, inferring, generalizing, predicting or classifying. Yet these are the language functions which are related to learning and the development of cognition; they occur in all areas of the curriculum, and without them a child's potential in academic areas cannot be realized. (p. 3)

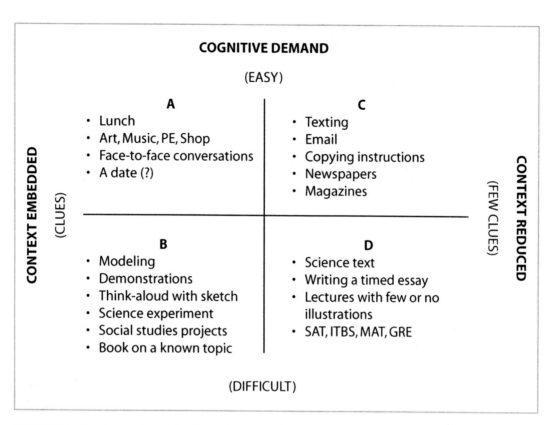

FIGURE 2.1: Quadrants of cognitive demand. Adapted from quadrants described by Cummins (1994, 2001).

Language learners entering our schools, at any age, will more quickly acquire the language of social communication than that of school. They want to interact with their peers. As teachers we need to be cognizant that bilingual students exhibiting fluent social communication are not necessarily proficient in the English language. Take away the context-embedded social situation or change the topic and the person who appeared fluent may be completely lost. When students can make complex meanings with language alone, with no contextual cues, they are demonstrating high academic language proficiency, and that is the level of proficiency our students need to successfully navigate schools from preK–12 and through higher education. But for them to get there, we must embed and support our instruction.

Implications for Teachers

The quadrants in Figure 2.1 illustrate what I was missing in my early years of instruction. I wasn't considering the language proficiency of my students or thinking about how I could provide language support through the context of my instruction so that my students could focus on the content of my instruction. Language support is an element of instruction that teachers can manipulate. We can make difficult concepts more accessible when we increase our contextual support, embedding the learning in things such as pictures; real objects or imitations of real objects, sometimes called "realia"; and even the students' home language.

When a lesson doesn't go well for language learners in my class, I can use the quadrant chart to help me figure out what I could add to or change in my instruction to help make the concepts more accessible. Our instruction needs to be situated in quadrant B of Figure 2.1 for optimal linguistic, cognitive, and academic growth to occur—where the context supports both the language and the learning of our students, even when the cognitive load is heavy. We want to provide our language learners with the cognitively demanding learning they need to thrive in academic settings and to move forward to meet standards and benchmarks. We don't want to change the standards for content learning for English language learners; rather, we want to change the context and the support in which instruction and expectations are presented so that our students can focus on cognitive demands. Unfortunately, academic settings are often situated in quadrant D, where the cognitive load is heavy and the context does little to support learning.

If successful teaching of language learners needs to include attention to both context and cognitive demands, then we need to discuss important considerations for establishing an appropriate context while also successfully supporting the cognitive demands for a range of bilingual students.

Context Considerations

Miguel was the first Spanish-speaking student in my husband's fourth-grade classroom. With the best of intentions, Mr. Buly asked Miguel if *edición* meant the same in Spanish as it did in English—"edition." It does. However, Miguel clammed up, so Mr. Buly dropped the subject. Later, when Mr. Buly went back to talk with Miguel, Miguel explained that he did not want the other students to know he spoke Spanish. Miguel perceived his first language as a hindrance rather than an asset to learning a second language. His attitude likely had its roots in caring teachers and others who didn't understand the critical role that first language acquisition plays in developing high levels of proficiency in additional languages. Miguel needed to know that his knowledge of Spanish was valuable. He also needed a teacher who understood how feeling safe and able to take risks helps students access both language and content.

The affective filter hypothesis described by Krashen (1994) helps teachers understand how the connection between language acquisition and the context in which it is acquired influences students' sense of well-being. For optimal language acquisition to occur, learners need motivation, self-esteem, and a lack of anxiety so that they do not raise their affective filter, which is a mental block that prevents or slows down language acquisition (or any other learning). To keep the affective filter low, teachers need to provide a safe and motivating environment. Say you're driving through a country where you don't speak the language and few speak English. You need to stop for a restroom. Ahead you see a restaurant and you feel a sense of relief. You walk into the restaurant and ask for a bathroom. The cashier glances up, motions to another person in the restaurant, and they start to laugh, as if you have spoken gibberish. Your sense of relief turns to anxiety as your face flushes.

Implications for Teachers

We can be more effective teachers if we think about and make connections with the funds of knowledge that each student brings when he or she walks through the door of our classroom.

To lower the affective filter and help our students in the difficult process of second language acquisition in a safe environment, we can work on accepting, affirming, celebrating, and connecting with the language, historical, political, and cultural backgrounds of our language learners. This does not mean we have to be experts in each student's culture or understand all the languages our students speak, but we do have to understand the importance of the rich and varied knowledge our students bring. As mainstream classroom teachers, we often know very little about the lives of our students outside of school. As we work to know our students better, we will learn about and better understand the rich cultural and cognitive resources each brings to the classroom; their life experiences have given them knowledge we may not realize. Luis Moll and his colleagues (González, Moll, & Amanti, 2005; Moll, Amanti, Neff, & González, 1992) call the knowledge from these life experiences "funds of knowledge." Many educators would argue that what children bring of themselves to school constitutes the base of what instruction needs to be.

To know our students, we need to take a nonevaluative, nonjudgmental stance.
Some examples of funds of knowledge that come from beliefs and practices include the knowledge that farmworkers might have about certain crops

or animals, or the knowledge older siblings might have about caring for children, or knowledge about education or religion. We also have funds of knowledge from our life experiences, and our knowledge as well as our students' can affect how we perceive situations. González et al. (2005) provide some ideas for getting to know our students' and their families' funds of knowledge. We may not always agree with what we hear, what we see, or what others believe or practice, but our role is to understand how others make sense of their lives, not to pass judgment. As teachers, we need to be good listeners and interested observers. We need to pay attention to details. We need to note our observations but not add labels. If we ask respectful questions and listen to the answers with the intent to learn more about others, we can successfully begin to know much more about the funds of knowledge our students bring to the classroom.

Looking at each student as a person who brings knowledge to the classroom and making a point of learning about each child's individual funds of knowledge is a powerful way to make connections with students. Some teachers try to visit the families of their students. When possible, I urge teachers to make at least one home visit to at least one family in the community, to spend time driving around the neighborhoods of their students, and to accept invitations from students to family events when possible. Culturally responsive instruction can develop through connecting with this knowledge in the classroom. One caution, however: don't overgeneralize from one student's knowledge; it may or may not be representative of a larger culture or community. See Moll et al. (1992) for an example of how a teacher might go into a household to learn more about a child's background.

Affirm students' home languages and model taking risks by learning a few phrases from the home language of each student in the classroom.
You might start the academic day by having each student say "good morning" in the language of the student's choice. Another affirmation is to have the entire class learn some phrases in a new language, modeling that we all learn languages and as we do, we all show language confusion and errors. A classroom teacher who understands how important it is to create a strong and safe sense of community will help to lower students' affective filters, and that will result in a classroom in which students feel safer to take the risks needed to learn a language.

Recognize that an accent is not an error.
Many language learners will read and speak English with what native English speakers consider an accent, and will often make what seem to be

simple errors not only as they are learning English but throughout their lives (Kuhl, 2004). One public figure with a strong accent is Henry Kissinger, the German-born former United States Secretary of State, among other diplomatic appointments, and recipient of the Nobel Peace Prize. In spite of living in the United States for many years, speaking fluent English, and obviously understanding English incredibly well, Kissinger continued to have a strong accent from his native German language. Accents are not indicators of intelligence or language proficiency. They have to do with pronunciation and the influence of our first language and the specific areas we grew up in.

Students need to see themselves in the materials we use for demonstrations.
We can further bring in the culture, interests, and experiences of our students by making sure that every student sees himself or herself in our classroom read-alouds, classroom libraries, and school libraries. When students make a personal connection with academic materials, they are more apt to be engaged and to take risks. This doesn't necessarily mean that every language group needs to be represented in all materials, but instead that students see their cultures in at least some of the materials. Culture is more than language, race, or ethnicity. Consider, for example, pop culture, adolescent culture, or the culture of your local area or setting. Books should be age appropriate, content appropriate, or setting appropriate, or a combination. Teachers need to promote *each* of these books by reading a bit to the class or giving brief book talks to show that all cultures are valued.

When we include texts and materials that connect with our students lives, we are selecting "culturally relevant" materials. Relevant texts go beyond ethnicity to include characters, situations, and environments in which students see themselves, their families, and/or their social and economic situations. Culture also includes pop culture relevant to students' lives, times, and settings (Allington, 2011). Yvonne and David Freeman (2009) have devised a simple rubric that teachers and students can use to help consider the cultural relevance of texts for particular readers (see Figure 2.2). Questions include those such as "Are the characters in the story like you and your family?" The authors also discuss the use of this rubric in their article "Connecting Students to Culturally Relevant Texts" (Y. S. Freeman & D. Freeman, 2004). Modifying and creating questions that focus on your students will help you select culturally relevant materials appropriate for your specific classroom.

Students from in the same country may speak different languages
A common assumption is that students who come from the same country will speak the same language. This is simply not true. The Pacific

1.	Are the characters in the story like you and your family?			
	Just like us...Not at all			
	4	3	2	1
2.	Have you lived in or visited places like those in the story?			
	Yes ....No			
	4	3	2	1
3.	Could this story take place this year?			
	Yes ....No			
	4	3	2	1
4.	How close do you think the main characters are to you in age?			
	Very close...Not close at all			
	4	3	2	1
5.	Are there main characters in the story who are boys [for boys] or girls [or girls]?			
	Yes ....No			
	4	3	2	1
6.	Do the characters talk like you and your family do?			
	Yes ....No			
	4	3	2	1
7.	How often do you read stories like these?			
	Often..Never			
	4	3	2	1
8.	Have you ever had an experience like one described in this story?			
	Yes ....No			
	4	3	2	1

FIGURE 2.2: The Freemans' cultural relevance texts rubric.

Northwest, for example, has experienced an increase in the number of students from the Michoacán region of Mexico. Some of the students from this region speak one of several indigenous languages at home, Spanish in the wider community, and beginning English in school. In one school where I have worked, teachers couldn't understand why students whose parents had been in the United States for years and who had emigrated from Mexico didn't seem to understand Spanish. But when the parents came to school to pick up their children, the teachers discovered that the parents spoke neither Spanish nor English fluently; rather, they were fluent speakers of Purépecha, one of the more than 200 distinct indigenous languages of Mexico and the most common indigenous language spoken in Michoacán. Teachers realized that what they had in their classrooms were really trilingual students. Together, we did a quick Internet search using the word *Michoacán* and the phrase "indigenous languages" to add to our understanding. We found that

[a]ccording to the 2000 census, the population of persons five years and more who spoke indigenous languages in the state of Michoacán totaled 121,849 individuals. The most common indigenous languages in Michoacán are: Purépecha (109,361), Náhuatl (4,706), Mazahua (4,338), Otomí (732), Mixteco (720), and Zapoteco (365). (Schmal, 1994)

This new information about language diversity helped us realize that we can never assume that the language a student in our school speaks is a first or strongest language. Nor can we assume that we understand the culture of a child based solely on country of origin. When talking with parents, through either an official translator or a community translator, it is critical to find out not just where your students are from but what language they speak at home. To complicate matters, in our experience families will often indicate that Spanish is a home language even when they speak an indigenous language in the home. Therefore, working with an interpreter to devise questions related to language use is helpful. Following are examples of questions often found on school enrollment forms. These are written for the student to answer, but they can be rewritten for parents to answer or to be used in any way that helps you know the student:

- Is English your first language?
- Can you speak another language? If yes, what language?
- What language do you speak most often with your friends?
- What language do you speak most often with your family?
- Can you read? If yes, what language?
- Can you write? If yes, what language?
- Have you gone to school before? Where?

Cognitive Considerations

Although establishing your classroom as a safe context is important, it is not enough. Jose was new to a school, having just moved from Mexico, where he had been going to a private school. His English was limited, like that of several of his classmates.

However, his understanding of science was above the level of most of the other students, and his Spanish literacy skills were well developed. Because of his limited English, Mrs. Bertola grouped him with the other language learners during science time. He had really enjoyed science in Mexico, but he didn't feel like he was learning anything new about science or about language in this American sixth-grade classroom. He found himself spending most of his time trying to help his peers learn the content, and he was frustrated.

Instructional Considerations

To reach bilingual learners and move them forward, we need to connect with what they already know.

Bilingual learners have knowledge in more than one language, and the knowledge they are able to express can be very different depending on the language in which it was learned. We need to know what each student brings to our classroom so that we can tap into their various funds of knowledge (González et al., 2005; Moll et al., 1992). If students have prior schooling, we need to know about that and help them move beyond content they already know. Conceptual knowledge developed in one language helps to make input in another language comprehensible. For example, if a student already understands the concepts of "immigration" or "migration" in a home language, the student simply has to acquire the labels for these terms in English. It is a far more difficult task, however, if the student has to acquire both the label and the concept in the second language.

Identifying students' cognitive abilities is challenging because a student's level of language knowledge in one language may be masking knowledge expressible in another language.

As literacy teachers, we can all identify with the surprise we felt the first time we saw a struggling reader suddenly excel when the materials or topic related to that student's strengths or interests. Think about the student who hasn't been engaged with books finding a book on skateboarding, an out-of-school passion. Or consider the science teacher who finds that the student struggling with the work in the text is extremely talented in the laboratory, where the materials support the concepts. All of our students will develop literacy skills more easily and rapidly if we can identify their level of literacy in both their home language and English, and if we connect them to materials and topics they are already familiar with or care about.

Some students come to school reading and writing in a first language but not yet in English. These students have an advantage because their first language literacy will help them learn English. They have already learned the critical part of reading and writing: that there is a way to express words in symbols and a way to make meaning from the symbols produced by others. They already understand that the marks on a page have a communicative purpose.

Equally likely, we will have students who speak a home language proficiently but have not had the opportunity to learn to read or write in that language and have not yet learned any English. The stronger the students' oral proficiency in their home language, including vocabulary and conceptual understanding, the easier it should be to acquire English.

Then there are those who read or write fairly proficiently in English, having studied in school, but who have not had the opportunity to engage in conversation with native speakers of English. These students will likely excel in academic English and also quickly acquire oral proficiency if they have lots of meaningful interaction with native speakers.

Some students might come from families that have recently emigrated from a country where the home language has been discounted, and parents expect their children to speak only English in the home. These students are in danger of ending up without fluent literacy in either a home language or in English because they have not had the opportunity to richly develop language and the vocabulary and knowledge that come with it.

Assess acquisition of reading, writing, and speaking in every language the student speaks.
Assessment will be key to understanding all of the cognitive skills our students bring to our classrooms. What this means for the teacher of language learners is that whenever possible, you need to assess the acquisition of reading, writing, and speaking in every language the student speaks. This is not, of course, an easy task for the classroom teacher. However, with a little creativity we can find out a great deal about most students with the help of a bilingual teacher, instructional assistant, parent, or concerned other. Community groups and churches can often assist with locating fluent bilingual speakers if assistance is needed. For the purposes of this chapter, I focus on assessing English acquisition. While assessing language skills may not accurately represent the entire child, it provides a solid starting point and can make a difference going forward.

Consider where students are in their acquisition of the English language.
You can find more than one document describing the levels of English acquisition. In fact, many states have developed their own criteria for

English language acquisition. States often align levels with those identified by national organizations. Teachers of English to Speakers of Other Languages (TESOL) published a document describing language acquisition in five levels. The following list provides an introduction to different stages in students' acquisition of English. A complete description of each level can be found on the TESOL website at http://www.tesol.org/s_tesol/sec_document.asp?CID=281&DID=13323#levels.

Level 1—Starting: Students initially have limited or no understanding of English. They respond nonverbally to simple commands, statements, and questions.

Level 2—Emerging: Students can understand phrases and short sentences.

Level 3—Developing: Students understand more complex speech but still may require some repetition. Grammatical errors are still frequent.

Level 4—Expanding: Students' language skills are adequate for most day-to-day communication needs.

Level 5—Bridging: Students can express themselves fluently and spontaneously on a wide range of topics.

With a better understanding of our language learners' current skills in English, we are better able to support access to our curriculum.

Our knowledge of students' English proficiency provides guidance in developing appropriate instruction that will engage students. Mary Cappellini, in *Balancing Reading and Language Learning* (2005), suggests that when a text is difficult for a student, we must first ask *why* the material is difficult. Perhaps the student's content comprehension is higher than his or her ability to form sentences in English—in other words, the student's cognitive ability in the content may be higher than his or her current cognitive ability to express understanding in the language. Cappellini offers the example of giving a book written in past tense to a student who is successfully using English in the present tense. The student may struggle with this book. Yet a book covering the same content at the same assessed reading level written in present tense might be very easy for this same student.

The question we need to ask is whether the book is too hard or whether the language structure in this particular text is too advanced. Even small insights into a student's cognitive ability can help us target and support appropriate instruction.

Watch for what students "use but confuse" throughout the day (Bear, Helman, Invernizzi, Templeton, & Johnston, 2007).

Assessing English reading, writing, and communication can and should occur throughout the day in every content area, not just during the literacy block. Whenever students are talking or writing, you have the opportunity to assess language development in English (or in another language if you are proficient in that language). Notice the students' grammar, complexity of sentences, understandings in writing, conversations, and discussions, and keep track of your observational notes. Listen to students read to hear their pronunciation and reading strategies and, most important in terms of reading, assess the students' comprehension through discussion, retelling, and summarizing.

When we notice the language that students use but confuse, we need to celebrate because they are approximating and helping us select our next teaching point (Bear, Invernizzi, et al., 2007). For example, when a beginning writer starts to place a period at the end of every line on a page, he is ready to learn about sentences and where the stops belong. When a language learner is confusing the pronouns *he* and *she*, the learner is ready to focus on the difference. When a beginning writer adds an *e* to the end of most words, the writer is ready to learn more about silent *e*. With this kind of information, we are ready to teach.

Applying Theory and Research in Our Literacy Workshop Instruction

When planning instruction that involves language learners, teachers need to consider all the cognitive demands, including language demands, and the context in which the instruction will occur. The professional development for ESL and mainstream classroom teachers that has occurred over the years through efforts such as Project GLAD (Guided Language Acquisition Design) offered through the Orange County Department of Education (Brechtal, 2001), the Cognitive Academic Language Learning Approach (CALLA) (Chamot & O'Malley, 1996), and the research-validated Sheltered Instruction Observation Protocol (SIOP) (Echevarria,

Vogt, & Short, 2008) have helped mainstream classroom teachers learn and incorporate effective research-based strategies into classroom instruction.

The SIOP model is especially helpful because its research-validated protocol framework provides a way for teachers to maintain the specific cognitive demands and contextual setting unique to their classrooms while choosing from concrete suggestions for ways to modify or plan instruction. Equally beneficial, the protocol can be useful after instruction when things haven't gone as well as planned. I find that if a lesson flops, I can usually pinpoint the reason in an area of the SIOP that I didn't carefully consider when designing instruction.

The SIOP model is broken into eight components:

1. Lesson Preparation
2. Building Background
3. Comprehensible Input
4. Strategies
5. Interaction
6. Practice/Application
7. Lesson Delivery
8. Review/Assessment

Within these components are a total of thirty features to consider when planning with the SIOP. For example, Lesson Preparation is broken down into six more specific features, such as clearly defining, displaying, and reviewing content objectives with students. The SIOP model allows teachers to consider accommodations for language learners within these thirty features on a lesson-by-lesson basis. I have found a clear alignment between the components of the explicit workshop lesson and the thirty features of the SIOP. Both help teachers focus on the cognitive demands and contextual setting of instruction and both include the gradual release of responsibility. For the mainstream classroom teacher, however, the literacy workshop may provide a more manageable and familiar format for thinking about the SIOP in the mainstream classroom.

The workshop lesson described in Chapter 1 includes the eight components of SIOP in a format familiar to and used by many mainstream classroom teachers. When classroom teachers new to working with English language learners implement the entire workshop format described in Chapter 1, they can be sure they are providing strong instruction that focuses on one teaching point at a time, with appropriate language considerations, based on the same research that underlies the principles of SIOP.

The K–8 mainstream teachers I have shared this alignment with have indicated that it is helping them more effectively meet the needs of bilingual learners during instruction. And the ESL support teachers tell me that it helps them understand both the literacy workshop and how they, as support teachers, can help mainstream teachers support language learners within such a structure. Jenna Harris, a Title I intervention teacher at a bilingual school, used the analogy of a body to explain the fit between SIOP and the workshop model:

> The workshop model provides the skeleton to support the body while the SIOP protocols are the muscles attached to the bones that help connect everything together for the learner. They support the same key elements of good instruction, but sometimes a skeleton (or outline) is much easier to follow when instruction is taking place in the classroom.

Table 2.1 (see page 36) illustrates how I share the alignment between the seven components of the literacy workshop and the thirty features of the SIOP.

In the following section, I describe how the literacy workshop can be supported through consideration of SIOP features. As you read, notice how the framework of the workshop described in Chapter 1 provides the skeleton of the lesson. Cognitive demand (Cummins, 1994) is supported and reduced through a gradual release of responsibility. The teacher modeling and demonstrations, along with language supports, provide the embedded context that students need as they explore a new concept.

Connect/Purpose

The first key to effective instruction of language learners in a quality workshop lesson revolves around the connect/purpose of the lesson. As I emphasized earlier, students need to know why they are doing what they're being asked to do. This is even truer for language learners, who are grappling with figuring out what is imperative to learn and what is extra. Whenever possible, the purpose of a lesson in the literacy workshop should link to students' lives in and out of the classroom, providing context for the learning (Moje, 2006). It is imperative that you connect the lesson with students' funds of knowledge, or what they bring from their life experiences, and their interests (González et al., 2005; Moll et al., 1992).

Connecting with students' interests and funds of knowledge about idioms, Miss Gomm planned a unit of study for her first-grade class. Several of her students had asked her about various idioms they had encountered. Miss Gomm set a purpose for their study of idioms by linking to the idioms students had recently encountered in their reading and inquired about. She also pointed out how often idioms are used

Literacy Workshop	Sheltered Instruction Observation Protocol (SIOP)	How mainstream teachers might incorporate SIOP
1. Connect/ Purpose (What, Why, When)	Clearly state and display language and content objectives for students. Use speech appropriate for students' proficiency levels (e.g., slower rate, enunciation, and simple sentence structure for beginners). Emphasize key vocabulary and concepts (e.g., introduced, written, repeated, and highlighted for students to see). Choose concepts appropriate for students. Explicitly link concepts to students' backgrounds and experiences. Explicitly link past learning and new concepts. Explain academic tasks clearly.	Use *by* to help you differentiate between content and language objectives. Try the sandwich technique for vocabulary. Tell students why you have chosen this mini-lesson, what you have seen in their work or in the standards that suggests this is a good next step. Include the *why* this is important, link to the real world. Include the what, why, and when in your explanation.
2. Model/ Provide Information (How)	Use supplementary materials to a high degree to make the lesson clear and meaningful. Use scaffolding techniques throughout the lesson. Use a variety of techniques to make content concepts clear. Emphasize key vocabulary (e.g., introduced, written, repeated, and highlighted for students to see). Consistently use scaffolding techniques, assisting and supporting student understanding (e.g., think-alouds, models, visuals, more and less support as needed).	Show the students how a more knowledgeable other does what you are teaching; write in front of students; show your writing; read in front of students; show your thinking, etc. Formatively assess your students. If they are confused or don't "get it," step back, provide more support, provide a different example/model, etc.
3. Guided Practice	Provide meaningful activities that integrate lesson concepts (e.g., interviews, letter writing, simulations, models) with language practice opportunities for reading, writing, listening, and/or speaking. Emphasize key vocabulary (e.g., written, repeated, and highlighted for students to see). Provide ample opportunities for students to use learning strategies (also in independent work). Provide frequent opportunities for interaction and discussion about lesson concepts between teacher and student and between students. Provide sufficient wait time. Use group configurations that support the objectives. Provide activities that integrate all language skills (i.e., reading, writing, listening, and speaking). Engage students 90 to 100% of the lesson. Pace the lesson appropriately to the students' ability levels. Consistently use scaffolding techniques, assisting and supporting student understanding (e.g., think-alouds, models, more or less explicit as needed).	Formatively assess your students. If they are confused or don't "get it," step back, provide more support, provide a different example/model, etc. Try the sandwich technique for vocabulary. Think about tier I, II, and III words. Include turn and talk, try together, find a spot, etc. Remember 10-and-2! Two minutes to process for every 10 minutes that you've provided input.

TABLE 2.1: Correlation between Literacy Workshop and SIOP

Literacy Workshop	Sheltered Instruction Observation Protocol (SIOP)	How mainstream teachers might incorporate SIOP
4. Link to Independent Work (practice during independent reading)	Adapt content to all levels of student proficiency. Provide hands-on materials for students to practice using new content knowledge. Provide activities for students to apply knowledge in the classroom. Provide feedback to students regularly. Conduct assessments of student comprehension and learning throughout the lesson.	Actively teach, assess, and support students during independent work time. Actively move to students for conferencing and instruction. When it makes sense, provide small-group instruction. Formatively assess and take notes as you do.
5. Sharing (at the end of the workshop)	Use a variety of thinking skills throughout the lesson.	Have students share how what they did supports today's teaching point (select the students who will share during independent work time).
6. Close	Review key vocabulary and concepts.	Remind students of the importance of the what, why, and when of what you've taught.

TABLE 2.1: *Continued*

in books, in speech, and in television shows, as well as how idioms cross languages. Miss Gomm had collected several books about or with idioms that she referred to as she taught. Some of the students' favorites were Tedd Arnold's *Parts* (1997), *More Parts* (2001), and *Even More Parts* (2004). In particular, the students benefited from the colorful illustrations of literal interpretations of common idioms such as "it broke my heart." The students who had already asked about idioms had a purpose for learning. For others, the links beyond this lesson to other languages provided a real purpose.

Model/Provide Information

Talking at, or telling, students is the least effective way to reach our language learners (as well as most of the rest of our students). In the most effective instruction for language learners, teachers usually model or demonstrate the *how* of the teaching point rather than simply explaining. This isn't the same as simplifying. We need to make lessons comprehensible, to provide more context. This means less talking and more showing. Adding pictures and further modeling or demonstrating are particularly helpful for language learners.

A key to success in the modeling or demonstration portion of the lesson for the range of language learners in a classroom is careful consideration of the words we choose and how we introduce them. Slowing speech, carefully selecting vocabulary we might need to focus on, using pictures and gestures, and questioning what we assume students know about English and how English functions are critical considerations in reducing cognitive demand and allowing students to focus their attention on the teaching point being modeled. At the same time, we don't want to simplify our key vocabulary, because our language learners need to develop a grade-level academic vocabulary in English. We can use a variety of techniques to provide contextual support for critical vocabulary without pulling the words out of context.

One simple way to shelter key vocabulary is through a technique called "sandwiching," which can be used in any part of the mini-lesson and throughout the day. When a word comes up that you suspect is new or unknown to students, assuming they haven't already asked you about it, you can "sandwich" a known word with the new word. For example, when her class was reading an article, Maya, a fourth-grade bilingual learner, approached Miss Lopez to ask what the word *attitude* meant; she had encountered it in the following sentence: *They are planning to try to change the attitudes of children toward each other.* To allow Maya to continue reading the article, Miss Lopez sandwiched the word in the following way: "Attitude, how someone acts, attitude." Maya's teacher used words that she believed would be in Maya's vocabulary to explain or define *attitude*, and she sandwiched her explanation with the word Maya was interested in knowing. Maya was then ready to continue reading.

As you come to the end of the modeling/demonstration component of your workshop lesson, you will decide whether the students are ready to try, with guidance, what has been taught. At this point, it is critical to remember that asking students, especially language learners, questions like "Do you understand?" or "Do you know what to do?" is not an effective way to assess understanding or help students know what to do. When asked yes/no questions in a whole-group setting, students' affective filters are likely to be high, resulting in nodding heads that are responding more to peer pressure than to the question. A more valid strategy to check for understanding might be to ask students to explain or model the what, why, when, or how of the lesson to a partner and to listen and watch for signs of misunderstandings. If, during your check-in, it appears that the teaching point is not clear to most of the students, provide additional demonstration, modeling, or explanation before moving to guided practice.

Guided Practice

During guided practice, you need to pay extra attention to listening in and checking on language learners. Language learners should be able to discuss the concepts or ideas in the language that will best help them understand the teaching point. Asking for clarification in a language they understand well allows students to put more energy into the cognitive demand of the task at hand. Language learners might also be more willing to ask a peer who understands their home language for clarification than to ask you or another adult. You can ask the students to explain their understanding in English after they have clarified the issue for themselves in a language they understand more easily. Once understanding has been achieved, cognitive demand shifts

from the concept (now clear to the student) to the explanation in English. You can provide additional follow-up, respond to students' questions, and provide any further language or concept clarification needed.

When Mr. Gomez finished modeling, he asked students to turn to their reading buddy and discuss a character in their independent reading books. As Mr. Gomez observed the guided practice, he realized that Borysko, a student from the Ukraine who had attended the school for three years, was talking about a family member rather than a fictional character. A quick glance indicated that the rest of the students were engaged in their conversations about characters, so Mr. Gomez joined Borysko and his partner for a moment. Mr. Gomez affirmed that a member of a family is certainly a character, but that he would like Borysko to talk about a character in the book he was reading during independent reading time. Borysko seemed confused. Mr. Gomez had recently read *Zlata's Diary: A Child's Life in Sarajevo* (Filipovic, 1994) to the class, so he used this book and Zlata as another example of a fictional character. A look of understanding appeared on Borysko's face, and he then easily transitioned to talking with his partner about Fudge, a character in the book he was reading. After listening to the students share and formatively assessing from their conversations, Mr. Gomez moved from guided practice to linking his teaching point to independent work.

Link to Independent Work

Linking your teaching point to the students' independent work is a critical step in the gradual release of responsibility. To provide more support for language learners, model what the teaching point looks like in independent work. You might model in one or two of the books that students will be reading during independent work to show how the teaching point looks in that book. If the work will require writing, you might model using a student's independent writing. Selecting a range of student work to use as a model, including the work of those who are struggling as well as of those who are doing well, will provide greater contextual support for all students.

Mrs. Smith had modeled how to find "tired" words in writing and how to think about finding more exciting words. The students had practiced this in guided practice, identifying tired words in a piece as a whole group, and Mrs. Smith then wrote them up on a chart rack. With Maria's permission, Mrs. Smith now quickly demonstrated, in front of all the students, what this might look like with Maria's work. She read through a paragraph of Maria's writing, identified the word *good*, and circled it. She then brainstormed with Maria a few alternatives that would make sense in the sentence, returned to the word, and wrote the one that Maria chose above it. Mrs. Smith then invited the students to try this during their independent work time and asked that they all read back over the writing they had been working on the previous day before they continued with new writing. She also told them she would be moving around the room conducting individual conferences and would check in to see what tired words they had found.

Independent Work Time/Conferencing

Independent work time is especially critical for language learners. This time in the workshop allows you to check in with students, to clarify understandings, and to reteach if needed. It is perfectly okay to spend more time with some students than with others. Some students will only need you to check in or conference with them once or twice a week at most. Others may need daily conferences or small-group support. Giving more time to those who need it is appropriate because that is how we make our educational system equitable. We need to teach everyone, recognizing that some, especially our language learners, will require more scaffolding and support than others.

As you move around the classroom and conference with students, you will identify a few students who are ready and willing to share during sharing time. Your choice of students will be intentional because you are selecting those who have something to share that will reinforce the teaching point. If you ask a language learner to share, it is important to reduce the demand on the student's language skills by giving him or her an opportunity to talk and practice with you what will be shared. Having a chance to practice pronouncing words and to get one-on-one coaching in English grammar will help the student feel more confident when sharing in a second language.

In their conference, Mrs. Christianson and Livjot noticed a phrase that they both felt vividly described a character in Livjot's independent reading book. They talked together about what this sentence suggested about the character's traits. Mrs. Christanson asked Livjot if he would share what they had found. Livjot was excited about sharing. Mrs. Christianson asked him to tell her what he would be sharing. They conferred a bit more about this tidbit, which would take about fifteen seconds to share. Mrs. Christianson first verified that Livjot wanted to share during today's share time. She knew from this brief conference that Livjot was ready to share, that he'd had a chance to rehearse, and that he understood the concept. Perhaps most important, she knew that what Livjot would share would reinforce the lesson taught to the whole group.

Share Time

Share time drives home the teaching point. Sometimes the most perfectly executed teaching point falls on deaf ears, but the same teaching point conveyed in a student's voice or through a student's example makes sense to other students. This is especially important for language learners, who might need to experience a variety of models and explanations of a teaching point.

If you use partner sharing during share time, you should allow and even encourage students to clarify concepts in whatever language they choose. It's okay and, in fact, helpful for students to talk to one another in a language other than English if it helps them deepen understanding. Think of your own needs as you learned a language or traveled in another country. Think of a situation when you didn't understand the language spoken or when you were lost and then found another speaker of English who offered a comprehensible explanation. Such situations move you through a continuum from frustration and fear to relief and understanding. Clarifying with someone in a language you understand helps to both lower your affective filter and deepen understanding.

So as a teacher, understand that it is good for learning to have English language learners discuss concepts in a language other than English. At the end of these discussions, you should also expect the students to explain to you, and possibly to a group or to the whole class, in English, what they now understand, using a level of English appropriate to their current acquisition level.

If you expect students to discuss in English or share with the class, then it is extremely helpful for English language learners to have some starters or frames to use. The starter or frame can simply reword the teaching point, such as "I made a prediction that . . ." or "I asked this question as I read: . . ." Peter Johnston's (2004) wonderful book *Choice Words* offers many examples of language useful for sharing time. The following are drawn from his book:

Did anyone notice . . . (the frame would be . . . I noticed . . .)

Any interesting words?

Any new punctuation?

Any words that are a bit alike?

Any new ways of arranging words on the page?

Did anyone try . . . (the frame would be . . . I tried . . .)

Some new words they liked?

Some new punctuation?

A different kind of writing?

A different kind of reading?

Did anyone create . . . (the frame would be . . . I created . . .)

A new character?

In Mrs. Tyran's eighth-grade language arts classes, she wanted to have the students share with one another. She knew that many of the students were hesitant about speaking English with one another, so she provided frames for all of the students, explaining that this was language writers use when they discuss their writing, and she wanted to hear *all* the students use this language. Bilingual learners benefit because they have additional models in their native-English-speaking peers.

Summary

In this chapter, I have demonstrated how the workshop format provides a structure that can help support cognitively demanding instruction for language learners in a rich context. The workshop:

1. Aligns with theoretical research and validated practices focused on the instruction and learning of language learners

2. Provides a framework to help teachers get to know and embrace each student's unique language abilities

3. Provides a structure that allows time to provide differentiated instruction for each language learner

A Time to Try . . .

1. Choose *one* area of the seven primary literacy workshop components that you already use or are ready to implement. Looking at Table 2.1, consider how you are already including strategies to meet the needs of your language learners. What more can you add? I find it most effective to start with the area you feel most comfortable in, work with that area, and then add another. Just as with our instruction, our own learning is best accomplished one manageable step at a time.

2. Since we know that teachers need to help lower students' affective filters, take a blank piece of paper and on it write the name of each child in your class. Now write one thing that you know about each child as a person—things they like, background, home language, etc. Can you add brief notes about each as a reader, writer, and language user?

   a. Who did you forget?

   b. Who do you need to spend more time getting to know? Which traits or skills can you easily recall, and which might you investigate further?

3. With the same list, walk around your classroom and consider how the environment and books reflect the students in your classroom.

   a. Who won't see themselves? What could you add?

   b. How could you arrange what you have to be even more welcoming to your students?

Some Favorite Resources

Barone, D. M., & Xu, S. H. (2008). *Literacy instruction for English language learners pre-K–2.* New York: Guilford Press.

Brock, C. H., & Raphael, T. E. (2005). *Windows to language, literacy, and culture: Insights from an English-language learner.* Newark, DE: International Reading Association.

Cappellini, M. (2005). *Balancing reading and language learning: A resource for teaching English language learners, K–5.* Portland, ME: Stenhouse.

Echevarría, J., Vogt, M., & Short, D. J. (2008). *Making content comprehensible for English learners: The SIOP model* (3rd ed.). Boston: Pearson/Allyn and Bacon.

Faltis, C. J. (2006). *Teaching English language learners in elementary school communities: A joinfostering approach* (4th ed.). New York: Pearson.

Fay, K., & Whaley, S. (2004). *Becoming one community: Reading and writing with English language learners.* Portland, ME: Stenhouse.

Fisher, D., Rothenberg, C., & Frey, N. (2007). *Language learners in the English classroom.* Urbana, IL: National Council of Teachers of English.

Freeman, D. E., & Freeman, Y. S. (2004). *Essential linguistics: What you need to know to teach reading, ESL, spelling, phonics, and grammar.* Portsmouth, NH: Heinemann.

Gibbons, P. (2002). *Scaffolding language, scaffolding learning: Teaching second language learners in the mainstream classroom.* Portsmouth, NH: Heinemann.

González, N., Moll, L. C., & Amanti, C. (Eds.). (2005). *Funds of knowledge: Theorizing practices in households, communities, and classrooms.* Mahwah, NJ: Erlbaum.

Johnston, P. H. (2004). *Choice words: How our language affects children's learning.* Portland, ME: Stenhouse.

Larsen-Freeman, D. (2000). *Techniques and principles in language teaching* (2nd ed.). Oxford, England: Oxford University Press.

Moll, L. C., Amanti, C., Neff, D., & Gonzalez, N. (1992). Funds of knowledge for teaching: Using a qualitative approach to connect homes and classrooms. *Theory Into Practice, 31*(2), 132–141.

Reed, B., & Railsback, J. (2003). *Strategies and resources for mainstream teachers of English language learners.* Portland, OR: Northwest Regional Educational Laboratory.

Whelan Ariza, E. N. (2006). *Not for ESOL teachers: What every classroom teacher needs to know about the linguistically, culturally, and ethnically diverse student.* Boston: Pearson/Allyn and Bacon.

Reading Workshop and Considerations for Language Learners

If students are given text in a language they do not understand, then reading the text involves a double load: Decoding written language for the first time and connecting it to a language they have not yet mastered.

—CLOUD, GENESEE, AND HAMAYAN (2009, P. 36)

Twenty-five students are clustered on the rug, almost glued together. They sit this close so they can see the book that the teacher, Mr. Jeffers, is holding. They can also easily turn to talk with a partner. At the same time, Mr. Jeffers can see each student and listen in on the conversations of his classroom of students who represent various home languages. Seven of his students speak primarily Spanish at home, two speak Ukrainian, and one Punjabi. More than 80 percent of the students qualify for free or reduced lunch, an indicator that many come from homes where extra money for seeming nonessentials like books or time for trips to the library may result in limited exposure to reading outside of school. Mr. Jeffers asks, "What did you notice me doing as a reader when I read this page? Go knee-to-knee with your neighbor and talk about it." Mr. Jeffers's neck resembles a giraffe stretching from side to side as he works to capture pieces of students'

conversations. The conversations are in English, Spanish, and some other language I don't recognize but that I assume is either Punjabi or Ukrainian. All seem to be talking about his question. I don't notice side conversations, at least not today. "So what did you notice?" Mr. Jeffers asks again. "You asked yourself a question as you read and then you kept reading"; "You stopped and read a part again"; "You got stuck on a word but you didn't stop; you tried it another way"; "You answered your question and asked another one." Mr. Jeffers acknowledges each response and writes them on a list. "Readers, you noticed several strategies that I used while reading. These are strategies that readers use not just in English. Readers in *any* language notice when something doesn't make sense and use different strategies to help make meaning. That's what we're going to be focusing on over the next couple of weeks in Reading Workshop."

Shifting into Reading Workshop

Before moving to a reading workshop approach, the teachers in Mr. Jeffers's school were trying to carefully follow a published reading curriculum. The teachers, administrators, parents, and students were frustrated. Test scores were low, especially for the growing number of language learners in the school. Many students couldn't or wouldn't independently read the prescribed materials, and when they did read them,

they didn't pass the end-of-unit comprehension assessments. Teachers were using a popular computer-based online leveling assessment to determine the students' instructional level for reading. But the students didn't seem to fit the levels suggested by the program. The leveled texts still seemed too easy or too hard for different students, so students weren't getting practice reading at an appropriate level. At the same time, teachers realized they really didn't know their students as readers; they had been relying on a one-minute timed test of correct words per minute (cwpm) to identify students at risk. The primary diagnostic tools they relied on were the computer-based reading levels determined by computer-based tests. Trying to stick with the structure of the prescribed curriculum for all students didn't allow for a system in which teachers could meet the needs of each student. And the yearly test scores showed it, even though the students were reading faster and faster on their one-minute tests.

The next year the school decided to combine efforts and ability-group by grade level, assessing all the students' reading levels using an informal reading inventory. They decided to use the *Qualitative Reading Inventory-4* (4th edition) (Leslie & Caldwell, 2005) because it had been introduced to one of the teachers in her teacher preparation program. They hired substitute teachers to teach while they did the assessments on their own students. Everyone realized that to really know the students as readers, the teachers needed to be the ones who assessed their own students.

With the assessment information derived from administering the QRI, teachers felt they knew the students in their own classrooms better. They moved the students into reading-ability groups headed by the four grade-level teachers and the school reading teacher. So students assessed at a fourth-grade reading level were grouped together for reading, as were students assessed at all other grade levels. Now that they had readers grouped at what they thought were consistent levels, teachers matched the district-adopted reading curriculum to the grade level of the group of students they were teaching. Test results indicated some improvement, but not much. Teachers still were not meeting the needs of each student, and now they were even more under the gun because of low adequate yearly progress (AYP), a measurement defined by the federal No Child Left Behind Act. They realized that even the students who had scored at the same level on the state assessment of reading or on the reading inventory still had a variety of strengths and needs as readers (Valencia & Riddle Buly, 2004). As teachers examined the scores more closely, they realized that students who had once received ESL services but had been exited were some of the most struggling readers. They had to think about teaching reading in a way that would allow teachers to genuinely know each student as a reader and as a language learner. And as they learned more through reading and study, they also realized that they needed to better engage their students and be culturally sensitive, while at the same time providing effective instruction. They needed to learn more about the instructional needs of the many language learners in their classrooms who no longer qualified for ESL services but who obviously would continue to benefit from language support.

A group of these teachers volunteered to seek out alternatives to the current reading curriculum. They began to attend ongoing professional development focused on the SIOP protocol. In their first session, they learned about Jim Cummins's (1994) quadrant of cognitive demands and embedded context, which helped them realize that many of their students probably could read and understand concepts covered in class if teachers were able to give instruction in the home languages of the students. The students weren't yet proficiently multilingual, and they didn't sufficiently understand when the instruction provided was only in English without appropriate supports. At the suggestion of the district reading coordinator, these teachers attended a conference at which recent work by Lucy Calkins and her colleagues (2010) was introduced. As they listened, they realized that what they were hearing about was a structure that would allow them instructional time to know their students as readers, writers, and language users *and* include opportunities to better support the students who spoke a language other than English at home. They would come to know not only the level at which a student read, but also the strategies that student used when reading and what he or she liked to read. This new framework would help students feel more comfortable during reading instruction, and with the number of language learners the school had, more comfort would help lower the affective filters of the bilingual learners, resulting in students taking more risks in the classroom setting. Together, the teachers formed a plan to begin to implement reading workshop in their classrooms.

The first part of the plan was simply to listen to each student read out of an independent book and to talk with each student about the book while taking some notes about the student's reading skills. All of the teachers held a sustained silent reading (SSR) time in their classrooms. This was a 30-minute period during which all students read a self-selected book. In the past, teachers had usually read their own books or caught up on work during SSR. Now they roved the room, listening to and talking with each student about the books they were reading. All the teachers included read-alouds in their classrooms because they knew that reading to students at a level higher than the students could read independently provided many opportunities to develop vocabulary. Two of the teachers continued to read their own SSR book for the first 10 minutes of SSR because they believed that their students needed to see an adult model reading a book silently, and they liked to use examples from the book they were reading in their instruction. As the roving began, teachers took notes that included the title of the book each student was reading, why the student had chosen the book, and anecdotal comments about each student as a reader. It took two weeks, or ten sessions of SSR, for the teachers to finish meeting with their twenty-eight to thirty-one students. But when they did, they were amazed at how well they felt they knew each student.

This year, the third of implementing reading workshop, most teachers use the notes they take during conferencing in conjunction with state standards and district expectations to guide both whole-class and conference lessons. SSR has changed to independent reading. Before each day of conferences, teachers review notes on the students with whom they plan to confer. As they review, they plan possible individual, partner, or small-group lessons based on the students' needs and the grade-level expectations, focusing also on the alignment between their teaching and the core elements of sheltered instruction. They always include a content objective and a language objective, understanding that the content objective is what they are teaching (the knowledge) and the language objective includes the reading, writing, listening, or speaking skills students will need to demonstrate that knowledge.

When the teachers started this journey, they didn't feel as though they were reaching the bilingual learners in their classrooms, but now these students are engaged and growing as readers. Student assessments across the school show an improvement in reading scores. Even more impressive, bilingual students are also continuing to grow in their home languages because the ELL coordinator has helped teachers understand the importance of encouraging children to read and discuss in both their home language and the language of instruction.

Components of Reading Workshop

In my reading workshop, I break lessons into three components: procedures and routines, strategies, and literary elements. Thinking about reading instruction as three separate components provides a way to organize the critical teaching points without losing sight of the importance of teaching procedures and routines. Table 3.1 includes examples of mini-lesson topics for each component. The examples are suitable for the entire class, but each is especially useful in helping language

Procedures and Routines	Strategies	Literary Devices
What to expect in a reading conference	Thinking strategies we use when reading (ACTIVE list in Table 3.2)	Why authors use idioms and what they mean
What to do if you have a question and the teacher is teaching	Multiple strategies to figure out the meaning of unfamiliar words (e.g., context, rereading, predict and go back, ask someone)	Differences in structure between English texts and texts in the languages of our students
How to prepare to discuss a book	Choosing easy, "just-right," and challenging books in English	Typical elements in stories (e.g., setting, characters, problems, events, resolutions)
Where to go to select a book	Adjusting rate when meaning is lost	Text features (e.g., captions, headings, table of contents)

TABLE 3.1: Sample of Reading Lesson Topics Useful for Whole-Class Instruction

learners avoid common confusion and difficulty. Bilingual learners in particular benefit from the visual aspect of the modeling or demonstration provided in an explicit mini-lesson.

Teaching Procedures and Routines for Conducting Reading Workshop

Procedures and routines can be taught from the first day of school or from the first day of implementation of your reading workshop format. Within two weeks, you should have been able to meet with each student briefly at least once, even with a reading time as short as 20 minutes a day. One short conference on a book the student has chosen to read is enough to establish the routine for students and allows you to get to know and formatively assess a classroom of readers. Lessons in procedure and routines are important in any class, regardless of the language students speak or the age of the students. All of these are modeled, guided, and practiced to build a solid foundation for operating a smooth reading workshop.

Show Students How to Be Independent

The first set of routines must revolve around helping students spend meaningful time independently with books. This is essential so you can begin to confer. In *The Daily Five,* Gail Boushey and Joan Moser (2006) describe a step-by-step approach they successfully use to teach students to be independent readers. They call these the "10 Steps to Teaching and Learning Independence," which I've adapted slightly into the following list:

1. Identify what is to be taught.
2. Set a purpose and instill a sense of urgency.
3. Brainstorm behaviors desired using an "I chart."
4. Model most desirable behaviors.
5. Model least desirable behaviors, then desirable.
6. Place students around the room.
7. Everyone practice and build stamina (3 minutes).
8. Stay Out of the Way.
9. Use a quiet signal to bring students back to the group.
10. Hold a group check-in and let students assess how they did.

Following this ten-step model, I have taught procedures and routines to preservice teachers and teachers of language learners who have effectively modeled these steps for classrooms with various levels of diverse language learners. It works! And it works not just for reading workshop, but for any procedure or routine that needs to be taught in any preK–8 classroom, including setting up the writing or language workshop. To illustrate how they approach the ten steps, Boushey and Moser (2007) created *The Daily Five Alive!*, a DVD in which they model the introduction of independent reading using these steps. The model is filmed in Moser's diverse third-grade classroom, with many learners from various home languages. A key to effective instruction that I hadn't considered before reading, watching these steps, and talking with the authors is the importance of modeling appropriate and inappropriate behaviors. This type of clear modeling is especially important and effective for language learners, who respond with more understanding to showing than to talking or telling. Modeling provides the visuals that support language learners in understanding what is being taught, and visuals are an important language aid (Echevarria et al., 2008).

Be Clear about What Is Expected and What Will Happen during Each Part of the Reading Workshop

In Chapter 2, I discussed the importance of lowering the affective filter of bilingual learners. The clear and regular structure of a workshop format supports language learners because of the context it provides, allowing instruction to take place in quadrant B of Cummins's model of cognitive demand (see Figure 2.1). Once you establish the routine, it can remain the same regardless of who is teaching. So when a substitute or intern teacher is in charge, both the teacher and the students know what to expect. This is why the format of the workshop—starting first with the whole-group lesson, moving to independent work, and then back to sharing—is so helpful for language learners. When the context is supportive, students don't have to try to understand what is going on and they can focus their attention on cognitive demand (Cummins, 1994).

Familiarity with the format leaves you more time for instruction. In a reading workshop, students know that they will be held accountable for learning the skill or strategy being modeled. They know that if you have chosen to teach it to everyone, it's important. They also know, through the familiar format, that you will continue to work with each student until each independently demonstrates an understanding of the skill or strategy, even if their work with the material is easier or harder than that used in the lesson.

Model How to Solve Questions So You Can Teach without Interruptions

When I am engaged in a conference with a student or a group of students, I want that time to be honored as a special learning opportunity that is not to be interrupted except in the case of a dire emergency. To ensure this happens, I need to teach procedures around what I perceive as a dire emergency, and how to solve emergencies that are not dire. It's difficult to focus on a conference with a student if another student is tapping my shoulder or seeking my attention in another manner.

One of the first procedure lessons I teach is *what to do if you need me and I'm teaching*. We talk about what a dire emergency is in our classroom and about ways to solve our own problems. I teach students to put their name on the whiteboard if they can't solve a problem and need to talk with me. Between conferences or small-group instruction, I check in with those who have listed their names. I model what this looks like, and we then practice what this looks like. When we start using this procedure, I find that most of the students have independently solved the question or have forgotten what they wanted by the time I check in. This saves me time that I can use for instruction. Visually modeling this procedure for language learners is essential because they need to see that it's okay to have a question and that part of being independent learners is being responsible for finding an answer.

Another common interruption to instruction is associated with the words "I'm done." *What to do when you finish a book* is another critical procedure to model. In my classroom, reading is never "done." I often require some kind of accountability or response to a book or activity. I love reader-response notebooks, in which students write letters to me about what they've read and to which I authentically write back. Sometimes I might be asking for a specific strategy or skill in these letters. However, even with response notebooks I still hear "I'm done." I must teach my students how, when, and where to shop for a new book. This might include mini-lessons about knowing what your next book will be, and I should have included this in conferences with the students so they know where they're headed next when they're done with a book.

Include Families and Community Members

If you don't read in the languages that some of your students speak, enlist the help of those who do. Instructional assistants, parents, students from college or university language courses, older students, and community members are all possible resources to help with reading in home languages and developing home language materials for the classroom. One procedural strategy is to include family story nights throughout the year at which teachers provide the materials to make books and the families provide the stories by writing and illustrating together. As a result, classroom libraries grow in number and variety, family and community members feel involved, and home languages are recognized and celebrated.

Help Students Find Materials in Home Languages

Many reading skills and strategies cross languages. A beginning reader in English may be a fluent reader in Spanish who is able to engage with and learn from much more difficult material if it's in Spanish. Vocabulary and concept understanding may be easier to learn in the home language. When we have concepts that we don't understand and we're also trying to figure out how to read, the cognitive demand is high without contextual support (Cummins, 1994).

The content learned and the skills and strategies practiced in one language can transfer to English and help students as they acquire English (Bialystok & Peets, 2010). For example, if students have learned to read in an alphabetic language, they have already learned the alphabetic principle—that spoken sounds are represented by written letters. While they were learning this principle in their home language, they were also reading age-appropriate content and adding to vocabulary knowledge. They understand what reading is, so they now need to learn the new association between the spoken sounds and the symbols in English. If students have strategies for inferring or asking questions while reading in one language, they can use the same strategies when reading text in a second language. It's not only okay but beneficial for students to learn to read and to continue reading in their strongest oral language while learning to read in English (Bialystok & Peets, 2010). A critical set of procedural lessons revolves around showing bilingual learners how to locate or make materials in their home languages and why it's important to do so as readers.

Strategies for Conducting Reading Workshop

The explicit lesson example at the beginning of this chapter is from a whole-group lesson focused on strategies that proficient readers use when stuck on a word. Teachers often spend two or three weeks near the beginning of the year focused on this unit of study, using the following format: First, demonstrate what a reader does. To do this, think aloud about your reading and offer the students glimpses inside the head of a more proficient reader. This is very important for all students, but especially for language learners. Students are provided an opportunity to see what a proficient reader of English does. It's important to be explicit as you move through the unit about how reading strategies used in one language can often be used in another language. Remember that the big difference between proficient and less proficient readers in any language is not *what* strategies they use but that they have *many* strategies they can use. Whenever possible, point out differences between English and the languages of your students and how that might impact their reading. This is especially true for cognates and false cognates in Spanish, since the majority of bilingual learners in the United States speak Spanish at home. Following are several pertinent tips to remember when teaching reading strategies to language learners.

Demonstrate how readers learn to read and read to learn at the same time and how they use different strategies for each.
For language learners in particular, the focus should first and foremost be on comprehension and meaning while reading. As students are learning to read English, they need to be reading to learn. If a student is a beginning reader in English and is reading simple text, that same student still needs the content that other students are receiving if he or she is ever to catch up with the rest of the class.

Throughout our lives, we will encounter texts that we have to learn to read while at the same time we are reading to learn (for me, this is tax returns and cell phone manuals). This is just as true for language learners. Readers don't need to know every sound in English before engaging with more challenging texts. If they have support, appropriate text, and background for the content, they will learn more about English as they read. Language learners in particular do not need, nor do they benefit from, phonetic readers that provide no meaning.

Include graphic organizers and other prereading and rereading strategies to help make content comprehensible.
Learners must understand most of what they are reading to come to a deeper understanding. A variety of strategies can help you develop

students' background knowledge and support the content of instruction. Using supplementary materials such as graphic organizers, discussion before reading, preteaching of selected key vocabulary or content, realia, and prior experiences all help to enrich the context of instruction (Cummins, 1994; Echevarria et al., 2008).

Show students how the rate of reading changes depending on our purpose.
In one bilingual classroom I recently visited, the students' "reading goals" were listed on a bulletin board in terms of how many correct words per minute each was expected to read by the end of the school year. No attention was given to comprehension. All of the students, but especially the English language learners, had interpreted these goals to mean that "fast reading is good reading." While it is true that proficient readers tend to read fast, this is due to a correlational relationship and not a causal one. In other words, fast reading does not cause comprehension; rather, readers with high comprehension tend to be fairly fast readers. But readers with high comprehension also monitor their comprehension, adjust their pace of reading based on their purpose, slow down when they are not understanding, and use multiple strategies as they read.

The correlation between correct words read per minute and comprehension has often been misinterpreted, especially for language learners. The best-intentioned teachers erroneously use the cwpm measure as the *only* indicator of a student's reading ability. If the student reads at or above benchmark based on required words per minute, the student is considered to be a fine reader. This can result in what Sheila Valencia and I (2004) identify as "word callers." These are students who can identify words with relative ease and have good decoding skills but lack comprehension. Such students are especially prevalent among bilingual learners. Learning to decode a language is not as difficult as learning the vocabulary and language structures that result in deep comprehension. Therefore, students can be fast and accurate readers but not comprehend what they are reading. For language learners, vocabulary and concept knowledge have much more to do with reading comprehension than do correct and rapid pronunciation.

Explicitly demonstrate the strategies and benefits of bilingualism and biliteracy.
For years there has been controversy over whether beginning readers should be taught to read in their home language or in English first. Some bilingual models of instruction suggest waiting until a student can read fluently in one language before adding a second language. More recently, there is good evidence that students can effectively learn to read in more

than one language simultaneously (Slavin & Cheung, 2004). And as noted in the introduction to this book, early bilingualism may even reap rewards later in life by delaying the onset of dementia (Bialystok, Craik, & Freedman, 2007), so the earlier the better seems to hold true for bilingualism and biliteracy.

Teach multiple strategies.

Two proficient readers in any language might tackle a challenge in a text in very different ways because there is more than one strategy to effectively confront most challenges encountered while reading. Readers should be able to draw from a toolbox of strategies (Jimenez, Garcia, & Pearson, 1996); if the first strategy doesn't work, they can try another. This flexibility is the difference between proficient and struggling readers. When challenged, struggling readers often revert to very simple strategies that work sometimes but not always. For example, a reader might have strong decoding strategies, and when confronted with a challenging text, try to use only these decoding strategies, but not have any other strategies to fall back on when decoding doesn't work.

Proficient bilingual readers of English and proficient readers of only English use a variety of strategies to monitor comprehension, connect prior knowledge with the text, make inferences, draw conclusions, figure out unknown vocabulary, and ask questions. Many of the strategies proficient readers in any language use are similar (Fitzgerald, 1993). I have found the acronym ACTIVE, created by NCTE award-winning middle school teacher Barry Hoonan (2009), helpful when teaching students of any age about the strategies that good readers use (see Figure 3.1). It is important to model and demonstrate these strategies in multiple types of text and, especially for language learners, more than once. At the same time, it is critical to

---

A = Ask questions (Asking questions)
C = Make connections (Making connections)
T = Track what's important (Determining what's important)
I = Make inferences (Inferring)
V = Create visual images (Visualizing)
E = Create the "Eureka" moment (Synthesizing)
and
Fix-up Strategies

FIGURE 3.1: ACTIVE thinking strategies. (Acronym developed by Barry Hoonan, middle school teacher, Bainbridge Island, Washington, based on *Mosaic of Thought* [Keene & Zimmerman, 1997].)

always model, demonstrate, and talk about how although you're focusing on one strategy or one teaching point, as a reader you use many strategies as you read any kind of text. That's what good readers do and what we need to explicitly model for our students. We might be focusing on one strategy, but we still recognize that we don't use a strategy in isolation or for only one purpose.

Explicitly demonstrate how some strategies are specific to bilingual readers.
Language learners who are becoming bilingual readers have some unique possible strategies for reading. They can make connections or comparisons between languages, they can transfer understanding of concepts from one language to another, and they can access cognate vocabulary, depending on the languages involved. The languages of the reader determine the unique strategies possible. For example, cognates are especially helpful with Latin-based languages.

Teaching Literary Devices in Reading Workshop

In my reading workshop, I introduce literary devices because understanding the literacy devices authors use is essential if language learners are to develop deep academic proficiency in English. In this section, I share a few literary devices that I have found to be important for all students to know and especially meaningful for language learners. Jay Braiman, a high school English teacher from Brooklyn High School of the Arts, lists several more examples of literary elements and techniques on his website at http://jbraiman.com/mrbraiman/lit.htm (2007).

Literary elements are universal to a specific genre of writing.
As we read, the literary elements we encounter help us to understand the text. We find, or should find, certain literary elements specific to the genre we are reading. In the genre of storytelling, for example, every story has a theme, a setting, and a conflict, and is written from a particular point of view. Readers, especially language learners, who understand the elements of a specific genre will always gain more from their reading.

Explicitly teach that typical text structures differ from language to language.
The written texts in a language are based on what is considered acceptable or conventional by the readers who speak that language. Most written American and Canadian texts in English are either fictional or informational. It is important to explicitly teach the common structures and the various patterns most often encountered in these two broad genres to students who

are fluent readers in a language other than English and who are learning to read in English. Students who have explored text structures and their different patterns tend to have better comprehension while reading English texts.

Exploring the differences between how texts are written in English and in the home languages of the students is also helpful. If texts are translated well and retain the pattern of the original non-English text, they might have a different text structure, providing a way to explore text differences. For example, Spanish narrative is often much more circular in telling a story than most narrative in English. Whereas Spanish informational texts are often nonlinear, American informational texts tend to be direct and linear. In *Reading Strategies for Spanish Speakers,* Lenski and Ehlers-Zavala (2004) provide various strategies for teaching text structures. A way to start is through talking about and charting the structures of texts you read in class, explicitly teaching (through mini-lessons, of course) the various patterns that you and your students identify.

Include instruction in using text elements as an aid to understanding.
Students need to have explicit instruction in typical elements found in stories, such as setting, characters, problems, events, and resolutions. They also benefit from instruction in common text features such as headings, captions, indexes, and tables of contents. Further, eventually students will be expected to have a firm grasp of figurative language, including metaphor, simile, and personification, as their reading and writing develop.

Recognize that literary techniques convey meaning in a particular way.
Literary techniques vary and are carefully selected or included by authors to convey meaning in a particular way. Word choice, idioms, and alliteration are all examples of literary techniques. These have less to do with structure than with strategies chosen to enhance the writing. The "Figurative Language" rap in Figure 3.2 provides many examples of literary elements found in texts. I include the chant as an engaging way to introduce or review literary elements, depending on the level of the students with whom you work.

Literary elements are important to explore with language learners in reading, writing, and language workshops. Because elements are carefully selected to convey specific meaning and are often not used in daily conversation, they represent academic language and thus increase cognitive demand. By embedding the language in our instruction, we help our students to grapple with the meanings of literary elements in text. One simple and engaging way to start focusing on literary techniques is through a study of idioms.

Figurative Language Rap : Literary Elements

Chorus
Sometimes what you mean is not exactly what you say
That's figurative language, using words in different ways
Personification, alliteration, assonance, hyperbole
Onomatopoeia, metaphor, and simile

Verse I

When Sally seems to sit somewhere separate from Sonia,
Or Caleb calls Chris 'cause he's coming to California
It's called alliteration: that's what occurs
When you got the same sound at the start of every word
But when you've got a vowel sound that keeps sounding the same
That's a figure called assonance, yeah, that's its name
It's what I'm trying to define by providing this example
But I cannot deny that assonance can be a handful

Chorus

Verse II
A simile is something that you use to compare
Two unrelated things with an element that's shared
My mind is like an ocean; it's as smooth as jazz
But it's only a simile if it uses "like" or "as"
A metaphor is similar, but watch out!
Be careful 'cause you've got to leave "like" and "as" out
My mind is an ocean; my words are a river,
So keep your ears open as I continue to deliver

Chorus

Verse III
Now if the sun's smiling down, or the boat hugged the shore
That's personification, nothing less, nothing more
But with a buzz or a ding or a hiss or a roar
That's onomatopoeia that we're using for sure
Hyperbole: man, that's like a million times harder!
Take something true, and then exaggerate it way farther
Now you've heard this song from beginning to the finish
Now you've got some tools to draw your literary image

Figurative Language rap reprinted courtesy of Rhythm, Rhyme, Results (http://www.educationalrap.com) and can be found at http://www.educationalrap.com/song/figurative-language.html.

FIGURE 3.2: Figurative language rap: Literary elements.

Understand that idioms can be especially confusing to English language learners. Phrases such as "it broke my heart" or "lend me a hand" are examples of common idioms in English. Idioms and sayings exist in all languages, and they often create difficulties for language learners. Because they are second nature to us, it's easy to assume that students know what we mean when we use them. Especially if we use them consciously in class and explain them once, we tend to assume that students have mastered them. But it takes more to really learn idioms, especially for language learners. Recently in a fourth-grade classroom, the teacher introduced the idiom "on the other hand." When students were asked to include transition words or phrases in their writing, one student attempted to use this new idiom. She wrote "on the left hand," indicating that she understood the meaning of the original idiom, but the change in words made it nonsensical to readers. Her confusion provided a chance to clarify the idiom for her and others in the class.

Idioms are so familiar to us that we use them often in informal conversation as well as in academic discussions, and it's easy to forget how confusing they can be to language learners. When read literally, which many language learners first do, idioms often lead to a lack of understanding and result in a confused or frustrated reader. Yet authors choose them for specific purposes. So it's important to provide explicit attention to idioms and explore why authors might have chosen to use particular ones. Examples of common idioms that confuse language learners are listed in Figure 3.3. The list was compiled by Joe DeVoto, an international teacher of English who suggests that idioms be taught in context whenever possible. He has found that students will attempt to use idioms in inappropriate situations if the context of an idiom isn't clear. In the list provided in Figure 3.3, as a support for students learning English DeVoto has tried to use each idiom in a sample sentence that is as clear as possible about the intent of each phrase.

Language learners of all ages benefit from and enjoy adding to the idiom chart when they encounter new idioms in their reading or elsewhere. Adding a sketch or picture of what the idiom means is especially helpful because it provides that extra contextual support for language learners. Adding idioms and sayings from other languages expands the students' understanding while affirming students' cultures and languages.

A Day in the Reading Workshop

In Mrs. Scott's second-grade classroom, she links the importance of using schema, or background knowledge, to help understand what is being read, with a purposeful focus on vocabulary. In the next section, we'll listen in on Mrs. Scott's reading workshop. Notice how she uses the vocabulary that she wants all students to know. She doesn't "dumb down" or simplify her word choice for her language learners; instead,

as easy as pie means "very easy" (same as "a piece of cake")
Example: He said it is a difficult problem, but I don't agree. It seems **as easy as pie** to me!

be sick and tired of means "I hate" (also "can't stand")
Example: I'm **sick and tired** of doing nothing but work. Let's go out tonight and have fun.

bend over backwards means "try very hard" (maybe too much!)
Example: He **bent over backwards** to please his new wife, but she never seemed satisfied.

bite off more than one can chew means "take responsibility for more than one can manage"
Example: John is so far behind in his studies. Besides classes, he plays sports and works at a part-time job. It seems he has **bitten off more than he can chew.**

broke means "to have no money"
Example: I have to borrow some money from my Dad. Right now, I'm **broke.**

change one's mind means "decide to do something different from what had been decided earlier"
Example: I was planning to work late tonight, but I **changed my mind.** I'll do extra work on the week-end instead.

Cut it out! means "stop doing something bad"
Example: That noise is really annoying. **Cut it out!**

drop someone a line means "send a letter or email to someone"
Example: It was good to meet you and I hope we can see each other again. **Drop me a line** when you have time.

figure something out means "come to understand a problem"
Example: I don't understand how to do this problem. Take a look at it. Maybe you can **figure it out.**

fill in for someone means "do their work while they are away"
Example: While I was away from the store, my brother **filled in for me.**

in ages means "for a very long time"
Example: Have you seen Joe recently? I haven't seen him **in ages.**

give someone a hand means "help"
Example: I want to move this desk to the next room. Can you **give me a hand**?

hit the hay means "go to bed" (also "hit the sack")
Example: It's after 12 o'clock. I think it's time to **hit the hay.**

in the black means "the business is making money, it is profitable"
Example: Our business is really improving. We've been **in the black** all year.

in the red means "the business is losing money, it is unprofitable"
Example: Business is really going poorly these days. We've been **in the red** for the past three months.

in the nick of time means "not too late, but very close!"
Example: I got to the drugstore just **in the nick of time.** It's a good thing, because I really need this medicine!

keep one's chin up means "remain brave and keep on trying"
Example: I know things have been difficult for you recently, but **keep your chin up.** It will get better soon.

know something like the back of your hand means "know something very, very well"
Example: If you get lost, just ask me for directions. I know this part of town **like the back of my hand**

once in a while means "sometimes, not very often"
Example: Have you been to the new movie theater? No, only see movies **once in a while.** I usually stay home and watch TV.

sharp means "exactly at a that time"
Example: I'll meet you at 9 o'clock **sharp.** If you're late, we'll be in trouble!

sleep on it means "think about something before making a decision"
Example: That sounds like a good deal, but I'd like to **sleep on it** before I give you my final decision.

take it easy means "relax"
Example: I don't have any special plans for the summer. I think I'll just **take it easy.**

to get the ball rolling means "start something, especially something big"
Example: We need to get this project started as soon as possible. I'm hoping you will help me **get the ball rolling.**

up to the minute means "the most recent information"
Example: I wish I knew more about what is happening in the capital city. We need more **up to the minute** news.

twenty-four/seven means "every minute of every day, all the time"
Example: You can access our web site **24/7.** It's very convenient!

Reprinted with permission of www.teacherjoe.us. See also www.teacherjoe.us/Idioms02.html.

FIGURE 3.3: Common idioms in American English.

she provides visuals, explanation, examples, and support so that all of her students will understand schema. In the beginning of the lesson, Mrs. Scott does the majority of the talking and showing, gently and gradually releasing more responsibility to the students until they are independently using the strategy.

Connect/Purpose (What, Why, When)
(1–2 minutes)

Readers, we've been talking about the things that active readers like us do to help us understand what we're reading. [What] *One thing that readers like us use is schema, or what we already know about something. Schema helps us understand something we're reading.* [Why] *The reason it helps is that if we start by thinking about something we already know that's related to the new thing we're reading, we understand more about the new thing. We use schema, or what we know about something, schema, all the time!* [When] Mrs. Scott writes *schema* on a large piece of chart paper. *Some people call this background knowledge, what we already know, and it's what helps us to make connections.* Mrs. Scott adds *Background Knowledge* under *schema* on the chart paper. *For example,* Mrs. Scott does a very rough sketch as she talks, *if a new building was built on the corner, and it had a little cowboy hat over a hamburger with a speaker on the outside, with a driveway that goes past the cowboy hat/hamburger and then past a window, what do you think this building might be?* Kids say fast-food hamburger restaurant. *And what do you do?* The students say they would drive up to the cowboy hat and tell the speaker what they want. *Then what?* Students reply, "Drive up to the window, pay, and get your food!" And Mrs. Scott asks, *How do you know that?* They know because they've been to fast-food hamburger places. Even though this new one doesn't look exactly the same as those the kids are familiar with, they know how it works, and fast-food places work much the same around the world, thanks to the international influence of fast-food restaurants like McDonalds and Burger King. *Readers, that's how we use our schema, background knowledge, our schema to help us make connections and understand something new. Say the word after me, schema—your turn, schema. We do the same thing when we read. Let me show you how I use my schema when I'm reading to help me understand.*

Model/Provide Information (How)
(3–5 minutes)

I was at the library looking through books today. I picked up this one because I recognized a character. It's Clifford. Now, I know from the Clifford book that we read in class and because I've seen the Clifford television show that Clifford is a big red dog, he has an owner named Emily Elizabeth, he lives on an island, and he often gets into some kind of situation with his dog friends.* Mrs. Scott shows pictures she has cut from a second copy of the book. She posts these pictures as she talks because she knows that the pictures will provide additional support to make the material more comprehensible for the language learners in the class. *I see that this book has a picture of a big birthday cake and I see that Clifford is wearing a bib. So using my schema about birthday parties, what I know because I've been to a lot of birthday parties, I'm thinking that Clifford is celebrating a birthday and that Clifford's friends will be there. Hmm. Emily Elizabeth will be there and . . . something unexpected will happen because unexpected events—things—events often happen in stories about Clifford. Do you see how I used all that I already know about Clifford to help me think about this new book before I begin to read it? That's what readers do when we use our schema, background knowledge, our schema to help us understand what we're reading!*

Guided Practice
(2–3 minutes)

Now you get a chance to put your schema, what you already know about something, schema, to work! Mrs. Scott puts up pictures from *Sesame Street* and *Fiesta Sésamo*, the Spanish version of *Sesame Street*—there's Elmo, Cookie Monster, Rosita, etc. *Turn and talk to your neighbor about what you know about these pictures.* Mrs. Scott listens in as partners talk. She knows they all know something about *Sesame Street* because they had a *Sesame Street* video on during a rainy day recess the previous week.

Readers, I heard lots of you using your schema, what you already know—what's the word for that? Yes, schema, about Sesame Street *to make predictions about what was happening in these pictures. That's how readers make use of their, say it with me—schema—what they already know, to help understand what is happening.*

Link to Independent Work
(1–2 minutes)

Today when you're reading, I want you to notice when you use your schema, what you already know, schema, to help you understand what you're reading. When you notice yourself using your schema, background knowledge, put a sticky note on the page. We'll have a chance to talk about those sticky notes and how your schema helped you know what was happening at the end of our reading block.

Independent Work
(30–60 minutes)

Mrs. Scott dismisses the students for independent reading. She begins to circulate through the room, conferring with students about what they are reading, checking in on their understanding of schema with the sticky notes they're using, reteaching when needed, and reinforcing earlier teaching points based on individual language development.

In her conferences, Mrs. Scott identifies two students, Maria and Sam, who have used sticky notes to identify where they have used their schema about what they're reading to help them understand. In a brief conference, she has listened to their explanations of how schema helped each as a reader. Both seem to understand the teaching point, even though they are reading different books. Sam is a beginning reader; Maria is a more advanced reader but quite reticent about talking in front of the class. Mrs. Scott has asked both students if they would share with the class. Even though Maria is a language learner and reluctant to talk in front of others, because she had this practice with Mrs. Scott and has been affirmed in her accurate use of the strategy, she feels confident and willing to take a risk in front of the class.

Since this is the beginning of the year, independent reading continues for a total of about 20 minutes. Mrs. Scott knows that later in the year the students will be able to sustain independent reading for 30 to 40 minutes, but it's only October. Today Mrs. Scott uses the time to conduct reading conferences and take notes in her reading workshop notebook. This notebook has a page for each student in which Mrs. Scott writes down what she notices, what she taught or reinforced, and what she is thinking the student needs next. With a switch of the light, she signals that it's time to come to a stopping point and join her on the carpet.

Sharing
(2–4 minutes)

Readers, please sit with your reading partner. The pairings are carefully arranged—the strongest student in a subject is matched with a student in about the middle of the class, and those in the middle with students a bit less advanced. *I want to give you time to talk with your neighbor about whether you noticed a time when you were using your schema, what you already know, say it with me—schema—*Mrs. Scott points to the word on the chart—*to help you understand. Now, some of you might not have noticed when you were using your schema today and some of you might have been reading something you didn't know anything about, and that's okay. We use our schema, our background knowledge, when it helps us—not always!*

As I was conferencing today, like many of you Sam and Maria noticed when they used their schema, background knowledge, to help them understand what they're reading. Sam, would you share? . . . Maria, would you share?

As each briefly shares, Mrs. Scott asks clarifying questions to make sure the talk refers back to the teaching point. After Sam shares, Mrs. Scott asks partner A to tell partner B how Sam used his schema to help him understand what he read. After Maria shares, Mrs. Scott asks partner B to tell partner A how Maria used her schema to help her understand what she read.

Readers, I know many of you noticed when you used schema today as you read, and now it's your turn to share that with your partner. When you talk with your partner, it's okay to tell your partner if you didn't notice yourself using schema when you were reading today. If you did, be sure to tell your partner what you noticed and how it helped you to understand what you were reading today!

Partner B is going to start today. Mrs. Scott leans forward to listen in on the conversations. After about a minute, she signals the students. *Partner A, if you haven't had a chance, would you now tell partner B about what you noticed?* Another minute passes. *Students, I heard so many of you talking about how you noticed yourself using schema, or what you already knew about what you were reading, to help you understand!* Notice how Mrs. Scott has let the students know which partner is to begin and has switched from A-B to B-A so that each partner has a turn to be first. This structure provides language learners with both the expectation and the opportunity to share.

Close
(1–2 minutes)

Readers, today and every day when you're reading, remember that using your schema, what you already know about the topic, schema, can help you make connections and is one strategy that can help you understand what you're reading. Tonight when you're reading at home, notice when you're using your schema and be ready to tell your partner about that tomorrow! You might notice that you use schema even when you're not reading, and if you do, please be sure to tell me about that tomorrow!

The Reading Conference

The workshop format includes time for individual reading conferences. This time is critical for teachers to get to know each student as a reader while also providing opportunities for differentiated instruction. All students, but language learners in particular, benefit from this one-on-one time with a teacher. This special time is a chance for students to feel especially safe. Their affective filter is likely to be lower, especially if conferences are a regularly occurring part of the literacy workshop. The one-on-one conference is particularly essential in developing a rapport and relationship between teacher and language learner, thus providing an ideal way for teachers to get to know students as individuals and as literacy learners with distinct strengths and needs. When getting started with conferences, it's a good idea to familiarize students with the procedure.

Mrs. Scott introduces the idea of conferences in a short lesson by saying, *Readers, you are doing a wonderful job of building stamina, being able to do something longer, stamina, with your independent reading.* Building stamina was an earlier lesson. *Yesterday, readers were able to spend 20 minutes with their independent books. I am so excited because that means I can start coming around and talking to individual readers about your books during this time! I am really curious—I have heard a little bit about your books and I know something about you as readers, but I want to know more. So today during independent reading time you'll be reading and I'll be visiting with some of you. I'll come right to you. Today I'll be asking two questions when we confer. I'll write these questions on the board so that you know what I'll be asking today.*

What are you reading?

Why did you pick that book?

Over the year, depending on the needs of my students, I will add new questions to my reading conference. Figure 3.4 lists examples of questions, prompts, and activities I might use during a reading conference.

We'll talk a little about what I see you doing as a reader, and I might show you something new to try. Over the next few days, I'm going to spend time with each one of you getting to know you a bit as a reader. I'll continue talking with you all year, and I'll write down what I learn about you in this notebook. Mrs. Scott shows a blank spiral notebook with one student name on each page.

Once you have modeled what will occur in the conference, it's time to start. Students need to have material they will be reading independently, with choice but guided by you in their choice. I recognize that there are many strategies and

What are you reading?

Why did you pick this?

Summarize or retell up to this point.

What will happen next? What makes you think that?

Read a bit for me. [note miscues]

As you were reading, did something trouble you or bother you?
[note strengths, consider teaching points]

What other things would you like to read?

What's something you would like to do better as a reader this year?

Teach or reinforce a lesson if appropriate.

FIGURE 3.4: Example questions, statements, and activities for a reading conference.

philosophies regarding matching books with students. The important thing is that students need to be engaged with books that they can spend time with independently, practicing what they are learning, adding to their vocabulary, and allowing you time to teach. Once students are settled in reading (after you have modeled and they have practiced independence using Boushey and Moser's [2007] ten steps), it's time to move toward individual students, taking two or three minutes to talk with each. The following is an excerpt from Mrs. Scott's conference with a seventh-grade language learner.

Jose, from talking with you I know that you really like books about baseball. I'm going to make a note for myself here so that I'll remember, when I see a great book about baseball, to share it with you! A follow-up discussion later in the year might sound like this: *Jose, did you know there are also biographies, stories based on the lives of baseball players? Since we've been studying biographies, I thought you might be interested in _____ or _____. Which of these would you like to try next?* In this conference, Mrs. Scott reinforces the lessons on the genre of biography by guiding Jose to read a biography of a baseball player. Choice is included, but it's a limited choice, to help Jose move into this new genre.

As teachers, we observe all the time, and we know lots about each student. If we write information down immediately, we'll remember it, use it, and even be able to share what we have learned. It's important to keep some type of Record of Learning for each of your students. For my Record of Learning, I use a spiral notebook with a student's name on each page. I keep a separate notebook for each class that I teach. If I'm teaching seventh-grade language arts to four groups of students, I keep four spiral notebooks. You might, of course, have a better way to organize your notes and observations. However you choose to organize your observations and notes, you'll need to include the student's name, the date, title of the book the student is reading, and what you are noticing or what the student has told you. You might also listen to the student read a paragraph or two and take some notes on the oral reading, including strategies that you notice the student using or that the student might need.

In my experience, it is very important in all conferences to be transparent, observable, with the students. Early on, in a mini-lesson, I show them that I will always share what I have written with them. What I write in the Record of Learning helps me to be a better teacher for all my students. It shouldn't be a secret from the learner. Sharing what I have written seems to help keep the students' affective filters low while also leading into more discussion that clarifies and extends my observations.

The teaching point during the conference can be related to what the student said was troubling or bothering him or her. If the student didn't identify anything, then the teaching point might be reinforcing the day's teaching point or another teaching point that this particular student has been working on or needs. Don't let worrying about what you might teach stop you from conferencing! So—plan a lesson to introduce the conferences, letting students know that you are excited about talking with each student concerning what they are reading. You will be roaming the room and talking with students. Let them know that you will conference with each of them but that it might take you a week or so to meet with everyone. They also need to know that while you are conferencing they get the opportunity to continue their learning through independent reading.

Figure 3.5 provides an example of Mrs. Scott's conference schedule for her twenty-seven second graders. She uses the chart to keep track of the dates and the frequency of her conferences. She has found that using a new page for each month of the school year works well. Since she holds reading workshop four days a week, with specials taking the fifth, it took her eight days, or two weeks of her reading workshop time, to confer with all the students. She tries to have a conference with every student at least once every two weeks. Some students receive more frequent conferences, and that's okay; they need additional support. Looking at her chart, you can see that she confers with some students more than others. An XX indicates a conference with a student, with a follow-up check-in that same day. By noting the date, Mrs. Scott is able to look back at her Readers' Record of Learning (RRL) to remind herself why she checked in more frequently.

The notes you take are invaluable. The Readers' Record of Learning helps teachers consider what needs to be taught to whom. If most of the students don't seem to understand something, that tells me I need to plan whole-group mini-lessons. If only some students need a particular teaching point or appear ready for a particular teaching point, I can pull those few together for a small-group guided lesson.

In addition to using the RRL to help plan instruction, I use them when I'm talking with parents and support staff and when completing progress reports. In a discussion on independent reading (Riddle Buly, 2006), I included various conference forms and examples that teachers have found useful for their RRL.

Student	October 4–14							
	Mo	**Tu**	**We**	**Th**	**Mo**	**Tue**	**We**	**Th**
Sally		X						
Sarah		X						
Amanda		X						
Josefina	X		X					
Jose			X					
Thomas	X			X				
Hilda			X					
Nellie			XX					
Courtney				X				
Brandon	X			X				
Ashlyn				X				
Beau					X			
Siyad	X				X			
Ethan					X			
Moises					X			
Francisco						X		
Luna						X		
Estrella		X X				X		
Tomame			X			X		
Missy							X	
Eric							X	
Benjamin							X	
Jordan							X	
Jacob								X
Marley								X
Kyle								X
Salvador								X

FIGURE 3.5: Keeping track of conferences with a four-day-per-week workshop.

Summary

A reading workshop framework, with attention to the explicit mini-lesson, supports the cognitive demands of language learners in the mainstream classroom because of the way it allows the mainstream teacher to really get to know students as readers and thus to differentiate instruction. The modeling and visuals so important to language learners within the gradual release of responsibility framework support cognitive demands by providing a context-embedded instructional setting.

A Time to Try . . .

1. Refer back to the procedural, strategy, and literary lesson teaching points. Think about the lessons that you teach in your class, or that you have taught so far this year. Categorize your teaching points. Are you covering some areas in depth? Do any areas need more of your attention?

2. Are books organized and easy for students to access? A wonderful way to arrange a classroom library is to have the students do it with you. You'll probably want to use a variety of organizational strategies. Here are some places to start: favorite authors, current topics of study, genre, books leveled by challenge.

3. Try taking some notes about your students as readers, simple notes about who they are as readers, as a way to get started. My favorite tool is a spiral notebook with a page for each student. Some people like file cards clipped together. The key is to take notes about your students as readers in a way that works for you and that includes dates so that you can observe growth.

4. Consider your notes in item #3. Who do your notes indicate you need to spend more time getting to know as a reader?

Some Favorite Resources

Boushey, G., & Moser, J. (2006). *The daily five: Fostering literacy independence in the elementary grades.* Portland, ME: Stenhouse.

Boushey, G., & Moser, J. (2007). *The daily five alive! Strategies for literacy independence* [DVD]. Portland, ME: Stenhouse.

Boushey, G., & Moser, J. (2009). *The CAFE book: Engaging all students in daily literacy assessment and instruction.* Portland, ME: Stenhouse.

Collins, K. (2004). *Growing readers: Units of study in the primary classroom.* Portland, ME: Stenhouse.

Ellis, L., & Marsh, J. (2007). *Getting started: The reading-writing workshop, grades 4–8.* Portsmouth, NH: Heinemann.

Freeman, D. E., & Freeman, Y. S. (2000). *Teaching reading in multilingual classrooms.* Portsmouth, NH: Heinemann.

Keene, E. O., & Zimmerman, S. (1997). *Mosaic of thought: Teaching comprehension in a reader's workshop.* Portsmouth: Heinemann.

Lenski, S. D., & Ehlers-Zavala, F. (2004). *Reading strategies for Spanish speakers.* Dubuque, IA: Kendall Hunt.

Riddle Buly, M. (2006). Caught in the spell: Independent reading. In M. E. Mooney & T. A. Young (Eds.), *Caught in the spell of writing and reading: Grade 3 and beyond* (pp. 123–154). Katonah, NY: Richard C. Owen.

Sibberson, F., & Szymusiak, K. (2008). *Day-to-day assessment in the reading workshop: Making informed instructional decisions in grades 3–6.* New York: Scholastic.

4

Writing Workshop and Considerations for Language Learners

We need to teach every child to write. Almost every day, every K–5 child needs between fifty and sixty minutes for writing and writing instruction.

—(CALKINS, 2006, P. 7)

Mrs. Rosen, a sixth-grade teacher, was ready to start her writing lesson with her diverse group of students. Although the majority of students in this diverse school speak English or Spanish, some students speak Ukrainian, Russian, Punjabi, Mandarin, or Purépecha (an indigenous language spoken in parts of Mexico). *Writers, we've been reading lots about immigration in the United States. We've read poetry, historical documents, biographies, and realistic fiction to help us understand immigration. You've all started to write your own story about your family's history in the United States. As I was conferring with writers yesterday, I noticed lots of you using the thesaurus to look for*

a special word while you were drafting. That's one strategy, but sometimes if you stop while drafting to look for a specific word you can lose your ideas. And getting the ideas down is critical. We've also talked about how you can leave a space and come back or write part of a word. Another strategy is to write the word in any language you know; then you can go back and change it later. This lets you continue with your ideas, and that's the key to great writing, getting your ideas down before they float away. Let me show you how I use words I know in one language as a holding place for a word I don't know.

The Shift to Writing Workshop

The students in Mrs. Rosen's classroom and across the school exhibit a range of writing skills and strategies. For many students and for many years, the writing instruction in this school consisted of copying what the teacher wrote, especially in the early grades, and then responding to prompts provided by teachers as students moved through the grade levels. Prompted writing seemed important as practice for the students because of the prompts they were required to respond to on state assessments of writing from grade 3 through graduation. Students were taught formulas for writing, the most popular of which was the five-paragraph essay. Once students wrote and claimed to be done, teachers would identify incorrectly spelled words and grammatically incorrect constructions or suggest that students add more text. But when students wrote more, the new text didn't seem to add anything of substance to the piece. And the spelling! These students were still spelling many words phonetically, even in sixth grade. They just didn't seem to get English spelling rules. And they just couldn't internalize the grammar rules. The Spanish-speaking students were always placing adjectives after nouns, as if they were directly translating from Spanish into English. At this school, writing had become the subject that teachers dreaded teaching and a time of day when students really didn't engage.

Teachers didn't feel that they had an effective writing curriculum, and with an ever-increasing population of language learners in the mainstream classrooms, they worried about whether students had sufficient practice writing to prompts as required on the state test. Although they were using a book of prompts, the prompts didn't seem to engage the students. In fact, the prompts didn't seem to be culturally relevant, asking students to write about things with which they had no experience. For example, one of the topics deemed appropriate for sixth graders was "My First Concert." Another was "My Favorite Trip." Some of the students had never been to a concert, at least not the kind of concerts they had seen on television shows. They could imagine a pop music concert, but without the experience, how could they genuinely write about it, or provide authentic details? As far as a "favorite trip," for many of the students the most significant trip in their lives had been leaving a place they loved to come to a new country; there wasn't necessarily anything pleasant about that journey for them. The teachers felt as though the students just didn't care and the test scores showed it. More important, what were students actually learning? Something needed to change.

When the school district first implemented a workshop approach to reading instruction, students seemed to be more engaged. Even more important to the school board, reading scores showed a steady increase. The district decided it was time to expand the idea of the workshop to writing. Although teachers felt that they understood the writing process, they quickly realized they had not really been teaching students how to write, or helping students understand that writing is a process. As they began to implement a writers workshop, teachers simply gave the students blank notebooks and a time to write and then tried to introduce the process of writing. As students struggled to get started, the teachers offered no direction other than encouragement, erroneously believing that for writing to be authentic and meaningful, students should have free choice in what they wrote. But too much choice with no direction is not effective writing instruction, especially for language learners. Many students simply copied things off the walls, if they wrote at all. And the students who did write seemed to be writing the same kind of story again and again. Sometimes the stories never seemed to end! The students were all in different phases of writing, and the teachers couldn't figure out where or how to start instructing.

There was little evidence that students were trying new genres of writing, even though they had been studying genre in their reading workshop. Teachers realized that the explicit mini-lessons they designed for reading, lessons they carefully aligned with the research-based elements of the Sheltered Instruction Observation Protocol (SIOP) (Echevarria et al., 2008), were critical for writing instruction as well. They began to plan, basing their instruction on the needs of the students and the state-suggested genres of writing.

One teacher suggested that all the teachers form a professional learning community and together read Ralph Fletcher and JoAnn Portalupi's *Writing Workshop: The Essential Guide* (2001). As they read individually, they met together each week to talk about their understandings. They decided to implement the writing process introduced in this book, using the book as their scaffold as they tried a new approach. They started by deciding together on the process they would teach, recognizing that writing is not a step-by-step process; instead, writers move back and forth between different phases of writing as needed, and different writers use different processes. To support their language learners, these teachers decided to use the same language and process each year, extending students' understanding of writing processes as both their writing and their cognitive abilities developed.

The teachers then spent many days planning lessons to help students find topics and get started, including different ways to draft, as they introduced the writers workshop. Teachers were writing in front of students, showing the class how they chose topics. Language learners who had struggled to find topics to write about now worked with the teacher in guided practice to think about ideas before moving to independent writing. Once most of the students were writing, teachers continued implementing lessons around the various processes of writing workshop. They continued to meet with students who were not yet writing to help them find topics and get started. From there, they set a date for a first published piece. At first, this revised approach to teaching writing felt uncomfortable to many of the teachers. Still, even though teachers rarely had students write about a personal experience, the students were engaged. They loved writing; some students even asked to stay late or leave the class later so they could continue writing. The school board wasn't sure that writing workshop would be effective for the English language learners, but the students' writing and the anecdotal notes in teachers' Writers' Records of Learning (WRL) indicated positive growth.

The initial implementation of writing workshop happened quickly at this school. Perfecting the workshop continues today, in the third year of implementation. It has been a challenging shift for the students to move to process writing, where they have controlled choice with clear expectations and receive differentiated instruction. In truth, it has been even more challenging for the teachers, who are changing the way they think about writing instruction. This year the teachers' professional learning community is exploring Lucy Calkins and colleagues' *Units of Study for Teaching Writing* (2006) and Ralph Fletcher's *What a Writer Needs* (1992) and *Mentor Author, Mentor Texts* (2011). They realize they must consider the special needs of the language learners in their rooms before they teach any lesson, and they're thankful for the SIOP training they engaged in together two years earlier. That training helped lay the foundation for their solid work today.

Now the twenty-seven fifth graders in Mrs. Rosen's class think of themselves as writers. Some write only in English, some write mainly in other languages, and some are producing bilingual texts. This makes sense given the diverse language groups in this urban classroom. Most of the students are now enthusiastic writers with both qualitative and quantifiable improvement in their writing. They share their writing with classmates, family members, and other students. They write for a purpose and they write for their audience. They explore different genres and are held accountable for using what they've learned about writing. They continue to have choice, but the choice is controlled by the teacher. For example, they might have a choice of genre but not topic as they write across content areas to demonstrate their understanding from a science or social studies unit. Or they might have a choice in topic but not genre as they work to internalize the author's craft of writing in different genres. At other times, students might have no choice in audience but have a choice about what they write to that audience.

The Components of Writing Workshop

Shifting to a writing workshop is the first move that many schools make as they begin to change direction in writing instruction. Teachers in a school or district are often not highly invested in a writing curriculum and so are likely to be receptive to a shift in the way they teach writing. In fact, too often there is no official writing instruction at all. Students might be asked to write in response to an event or topic, or be given a prompt, but explicit instruction in writing—learning about genres and strategies that writers use—is rarer than people might imagine. Teachers, administrators, and school boards tend to be less invested in writing because huge dollars are not often spent on a writing curriculum, as they are on reading. Therefore, teachers who care about student learning may be quite willing to change how writing is taught to a way that more appropriately focuses on language learners. Table 4.1 includes sample lesson topics for each of the areas that I have found beneficial for all students, but especially for language learners, in the writing workshop.

Types of Mini-Lessons	Examples
Procedural: Making the workshop run smoothly	• Location of materials • What to do when "I'm done" • Having a quiet peer conference
Writer's Process: Strategies that help writers in each part of the process	• Planning in multiple languages • Finding a topic • Using different ways to prewrite.
Writer's Craft: Examining the qualities of good writing in English and in other languages	• Powerful descriptions • Strong leads • Using quotes • Patterns (circular writing vs. linear)
Editing Skills: Developing students' understanding of the conventions of writing	• Spelling • Ending punctuation • Subject–verb agreement • Tenses

TABLE 4.1: Sample of Writing Lesson Topics Useful for Whole-Class Instruction

Tips for Teaching Writing Procedures

Engaging English language learners in a writing workshop when they don't know what to expect often frustrates teachers new to working with ELLs. But the processes that native speakers of English and second language learners use are similar. As language learners progress in their English language acquisition, their writing will gradually look more and more like Standard English. Following are some specific tips that are especially helpful to the success of language learners when teaching procedures for the writing workshop.

Convey Clear and High Expectations for All Learners

Procedures must be not only explicitly taught but also modeled and role-played, sometimes in several different ways. Modeling provides a way to show language learners exactly what is expected, which allows cognitive demand to settle on learning about writing rather than on trying to figure out a new procedure. For example, teachers need to physically model for students where to get paper and how much to take at a time. In addition, before starting conferences or changing what happens in conferences, you need to role-play writing conferences with several students, including language learners. The purpose of role-playing in front of or with students is to ensure that students know what to expect. If they don't know what to expect, they will spend their writing time with one ear cocked toward you, trying to figure out what you are asking during their peers' conferences.

Create an Environment in Which Students Feel Safe to Risk Making Errors

Writing makes almost everyone feel vulnerable, and even more so if spelling, grammar, or vocabulary are a struggle. Language learners have as many ideas and life experiences to write about as any other student, but they may struggle to find the words and confidence to put the ideas on paper in a new language as their affective filter rises (Krashen, 1994). They know even before they write that they will make grammatical errors and have difficulty finding appropriate words and spelling them correctly.

It is important to recognize the risks you are asking your students to take when writing. Drafts must truly be treated like drafts and be a time when it is okay to try things and make mistakes. That will help lower your students' affective filters, as described in Chapter 2. Make sure your students have had ample modeling and guided practice before you expect them to independently produce final written products. Especially with language learners, it is appropriate to model and write in whole-group, small-group, and partner settings before moving to independent writing. Ensure that students are prepared to succeed on their own before sending them off on an independent task.

One way I have found to lower students' affective filters and get to know my students as people and as writers is through dialogue journals. In my class, a dialogue journal is a private writing space between me and the student. It is a place for the student to write to me about anything. I respond authentically to the content. I do not correct dialogue journals, but I might note what I'm noticing about the student's writing in my Writers' Record of Learning. My response includes an authentic question and provides a reason for the student to write more so that I can write again. I have had more success with teacher–student dialogue journals than with students writing to each other, although some teachers use both kinds.

I have tried using dialogue journals at different times of the day, but my favorite time is first thing in the morning, regardless of the grade. I have students spend the first five to ten minutes of class writing to me about whatever they like. This provides a way for students to immediately engage in a worthwhile literacy activity, allows those who are late to know exactly how to get started, and gives me five to ten minutes to meet individually with students. An empty notebook, provided by the students or me, can serve as the dialogue journal throughout the year.

As with any other independent activity, I model my expectations for the journals before students begin. I can modify these expectations depending on grade level and time of year. In kindergarten, for example, I might model drawing with labels. In eighth grade, I might model writing an entire page in letter format, with a quick pencil sketch at the end. I clearly state that the students' writing is not graded except in terms of whether done or not done. Instead, it's a time to dialogue with me. I also model a lesson around what to write when a student has nothing to write about. I ask students to write to me saying something like:

> Dear Mrs. Buly, Today there is nothing to write about. There is absolutely nothing to write about. Yesterday I did nothing that I can write about today. If I could write about something, then I would write about . . . well, nothing, because there is nothing to write about.

I model continuing to write about nothing for the length of time available for writing in dialogue journals. I find that many students will find things to write about as they write about "nothing," and others will give me enough "nothing" for me to write some authentic questions in response or to get a conversation started that will, with luck, spark a dialogue.

Honor the Time for Writing

Donald Graves (in Fletcher & Portalupi, 2001) is quoted responding to a teacher's question about how to teach writing if writing can be sandwiched in only one day a week: "Don't bother. One day a week will teach them to hate it. They'll never get inside writing" (p. 8). And how can anyone become a writer if they learn to hate it? Having regular time for writing is important for all writers and especially for language learners. Students need to be explicitly shown new things and have ample time to practice, and language learners especially need this extra time to practice getting their thoughts down in a new language. Writing needs to occur in classrooms where the time for writing is honored and respected by both teacher and classmates. Explicitly teaching students procedures for how to get assistance, how to conference, and other expectations is a critical part of writing procedure instruction necessary for a smooth and successful writing workshop.

Tips for Teaching Writing Process

Decide What You Will Call Various Steps of the Writing Process

Writing is a process that seems to move through different steps. Most people think of the steps as getting ideas, drafting, revising, editing, and publishing. However, teachers call these various steps by a variety of names. Lack of consistency from teacher to teacher or grade to grade can be detrimental to language learners. Your language learners need to know that *drafting* in first grade means the same, although extended, in second grade, and in each subsequent grade. So as a school team, come to a consensus about how you will label the various steps of the writing process. Students will advance further as writers if the definition of *revision* is consistent from grade to grade. I have found it critical to separate revision from editing. When I talk about revision, I focus on the content, ideas, organization, fluency, and voice of a piece of writing. Students work on and then check their own writing for various revision points that I've taught in mini-lessons. Only when a piece is considered "done" does the student go back and read the piece for final editing, which consists of spelling, punctuation, and grammar. Finally, if the piece is to be published, publishing is the time to decide about formatting, font, and how the final product will look. It bears repeating: have clear and shared definitions of *revision, editing,* and *publishing* in your school. Creating revision, editing, and publishing checklists (with graphics) as a school staff can be an excellent professional development experience. Figure 4.1 is an example of a final revision checklist and a final editing checklist. I modify the checklists based on our

---

Final Revision Checklist

Name _____   Piece _____

Date _____

___ I checked the work for clear and complete sentences.

___ I read the work for meaning. It makes sense.

___ I asked a friend to listen as I read the piece. It makes sense.

Friend's signature _____

Final Self-Editing Checklist

Name _____   Piece _____

Date _____

___ I checked the spelling using the spellcheck tool on the computer.

___ I read the work for correct word usage that the computer spellchecker won't catch (to, too, two, they're, their, etc.).

___ The first word in all sentences starts with a capital letter.

___ Proper nouns that name a specific person, place, or thing have been capitalized.

___ The title has capital letters where needed.

___ Each sentence ends with a punctuation mark.

___ Commas are used in any series of three or more things (apples, oranges, and pears).

___ Commas connect the parts of compound sentences.

___ Quotation marks begin and end words that someone says.

___ I reread, aloud, the document one more time watching carefully for all errors.

___ I asked a friend to edit. It's edited. Friend's signature _____

FIGURE 4.1: Examples of final revision and final self-editing checklists for writing.

focus for writing and on my expectations. Having a staff discussion across and within grade levels provides an ideal space in which to consider expectations for each grade level and to link to state standards. My personal rule is to grade a student only on those things that I have already taught or that I know were taught in previous years (and were probably reviewed in my classroom).

Help Students Discover They Have Many Ideas to Write About

We all have times when we're at a loss for words; we have an idea of what we want to say, but we can't find the words and we end up saying, "Oh, never mind, I can't explain it." Imagine how prevalent that frustration must be for language learners—so many ideas but perhaps not the English or written language to get the ideas across. So provide many lessons focused on how writers get ideas. (See the discussion later in this chapter under "A Day in the Writing Workshop.") The key, I have found, is to model brainstorming with topics that are culturally relevant, part of the students' lives outside of school. This might mean topics that are age appropriate, pop culture appropriate, home appropriate, gender appropriate, and so on. I also try to think of those awkward moments in life, such as saying something silly when you meant to sound smart or trying to learn to do something, that we all have at a certain age, or those wonderful memories of special events, such as making a new friend or spending time with a special relative, and model these topics.

Recognize the Educational Benefits That Home Languages Play in Learning English

Allow students to brainstorm and draft in whatever language they are most comfortable, even if you expect a final product in English. Allowing students to collect ideas and draft in the home language is an appropriate support for English language learners. Jose, in Mrs. Christiana's fifth-grade class, had just moved to the United States from Guatemala. Mrs. Christiana spoke a bit of Spanish but not much. Jose spoke lots of Spanish and only a bit of English. Mrs. Christiana had Jose draft his ideas in Spanish and then translate the final pieces into English. The result was a beautiful book of poetry, dedicated to his mother, with illustrations that showed Jose's talent as a writer and illustrator.

Allowing plans, drafts, and brainstorming in home languages will help students get their ideas down. Another valuable strategy for building confidence and helping writers get started is to model and encourage students to draw. This is especially powerful for those students who are emerging in English but don't have written literacy in their home language. With modeling, the following strategy has worked well for me: I have students write what they can in English, as much as they can, and then switch to their home language when they run out of words. This gives me an idea of what the students are writing about, and they are able to pursue their ideas beyond the English they have available to express them. I can engage in meaningful conferences in which I ask questions and support writing based on what the students have written in English even if I don't understand the second language.

During the lesson highlighted at the beginning of this chapter, Mrs. Rosen recognized that the students needed strategies to keep writing when they weren't sure of a word. She had introduced a variety of genres around the topic of immigration, engaged the students in thinking about their own stories related to the topic of immigration, and then supplied students with ways to get their ideas down on paper even when they have limited English. Mrs. Rosen showed her students how to use a word in a language they know when they don't know it in English, because the most important thing is to keep writing. Strategies that help students keep ideas flowing are critical for language learners, and they need to know that using these strategies is perfectly acceptable and appropriate.

Tips for Teaching Writer's Craft

I think of writer's craft as attempting to build the perfect birdhouse. We try different materials until we find the right ingredients or pieces. The contents of the birdhouse will keep the birds happy, even if it's a bit lopsided on the outside. Writer's craft is all about the strategies we use to communicate, like our figurative language or the way we use leads or words in a piece. Craft is the key to effective writing; it includes revision, and our language learners require extra support as they try to develop it, navigating the content of writing with the challenge of doing so in a language that is not yet familiar.

Follow the Student's Lead in a Conference

When meeting with students in a conference, I start with an open question such as *How is it going?* or *What are you working on?* and then ask, *Is there anything I can help you with?* This allows the student to guide the conference and also might help you figure out what the student is ready to learn next. And if other students are listening in on the conference, they will gain from the instruction provided. If several students seem to be ready for the same conference, confer with a small group.

Invite and Encourage Writers to Try What Has Been Taught

During a lesson, students should be expected to think about what is being taught and to try it during guided practice. Then students need to be invited to use what was taught *if it makes sense in their current writing.* Your invitation might sound like this: **Writers, when you are reading through your writing today and any day, watch for tired words and see if there's another word that might better share your meaning with your readers. As I conference with you today, I would like to see at least one place where you have found a tired word and tried another.** Sometimes students should make the decision about when to try what has been taught. But if a student absolutely needs to use what was taught, you can be more explicit and direct: **Jose, I see two tired words on this page. Here is one; what else could you use? Now YOU find another and think about what you could use instead. I'll check back with you in a few minutes.**

You might introduce several genres and then invite students to choose one genre through which to share an individual family story. This will help students learn about one another as they learn about genres. Although you don't need to dictate the genre of this particular piece, you can introduce and then expect students to write and then publish in specific grade-appropriate genres by the end of the year. A key to retaining choice is to have students decide which genre to use for each piece they publish. Students will be sharing writing in various genres, reinforcing your introductions to specific genres, as they complete each piece.

Teach the Buddy System for Revising

Teach your students how to help one another with revising. Buddies should first learn how to listen to the content of a peer's piece. It's easy to slip into editing mode, so I teach students *not* to look at the piece of writing when they begin to confer on revision, but instead just to listen to the author read so that the focus stays on content. Students should be taught how to respond with real questions and suggestions, which means providing explicit mini-lessons on dialoguing about a piece of writing and giving students the opportunity to practice. This is especially helpful for language learners because the dialogue can help the language learner clarify ideas in English, thus helping the student to write what he or she wants to say. Buddies who can ask clarifying questions in the home language of bilingual learners can also help the author clarify content and meaning. You can easily provide several mini-lessons and guided practice sessions on how to revise with a buddy. A powerful result of this is learning how to self-revise.

Include Writing Examples from across the School Day

Using books and strategies studied in the reading or language block enriches and provides deeper understanding during the writing block. For example, if you are studying idioms in language or reading workshop, bring that into craft lessons during the writing block. Or if the class is studying how authors write leads, bring in the leads found in books that students have read in social studies. Books and materials used for read-alouds, literature circle, or social studies, science, and math units can be reused as mentor texts during the writing block. A mentor text is a piece of writing that students explore as an example of a particular type of writing or aspect of writing they are attempting themselves. Having many mentor texts available for students is especially helpful for language learners. You can refer back to mentor texts during whole-group and small-group activities as well as in conferences, providing a model that language learners can consult during independent work. Sometimes the mentor text might be a piece written by you or a classmate. Whenever possible, include mentor texts written in the languages of the students. Consider having students write mentor texts in various languages for another group of students, perhaps those who will be in your classroom next year.

Tips for Teaching Editing

If writer's craft focuses on the content of a piece, then editing focuses on the "street appeal." Often it is the editing, including final presentation, that helps draw a reader to a book, article, or other text. Edited writing is cleaned up; it's neat, it's tidy, and that makes it easy for the reader to focus on the content. When a piece is not edited, it is easy to lose interest simply because it becomes too much work to get through. To explain editing, I use the example of buying a great dessert at a store. Out of all the desserts displayed, one might have absolutely the richest, most amazing taste, but because during baking it came out lopsided and not very appealing looking, no one bought it. For the dessert to be enjoyed, someone has to choose it. Likewise, if a piece of writing is not cleaned up, if it's full of editing errors or difficult to read, it will be overlooked regardless of the power of the content.

Teach and Reinforce One Editing Point at a Time

English language learners struggle with English syntax. Syntax is not innate, and it takes years to learn the grammar, structure, and spelling of a second language. Focusing too much or too early on correctness will inhibit the writer. When conferring with students who come from a home in which English is not the primary language, it is important to remember that we are conferring with language learners, regardless of the students' level of social English (Cummins, 1994). Language learners may use interesting grammatical structures. You can note these in your Language Record of Learning while conferring with students. Just remember that too much focus on spelling or grammatical structures with language learners, especially in the drafting phase, will impede their writing.

I remember a sixth-grade bilingual learner who was comfortable with and excited about writing in English in her journal. She wrote page after page, until I had a well-intentioned instructional assistant work with her. The assistant did what she had been asked to do for other teachers and marked every misspelled word, in red. The student started producing less and less writing, with little content and few words. Soon her journal displayed no red marks because the student used only words she was sure she could correctly spell. This resulted in correct spelling but stifled content because she was so focused on spelling.

My approach is to work on the common misunderstandings I see in student writing with the whole class during our language block. Many students confuse the same language structures and spelling patterns. I do hold students accountable for words they have learned to spell, and I do expect that students will carefully self-edit, using skills they have been taught and have practiced. Before students publish a piece, however, either I or a trained editor (who might be a student or a parent or an instructional assistant) will do a final edit. Whenever possible, this final edit is done during a conference with the student. If that's not possible, we discuss the editor's suggestions and corrections during a conference. I am very careful to keep editing in its place—at the end of the students' writing processes—and not to confuse the activity with revision.

Teach the Buddy System for Editing

Before buddies can help each other edit, they need to have participated in a content conference that focuses on writer's craft so that they feel as though the content has been revised to the writer's (and teacher's) criteria and satisfaction. Only after they have had a content conference with a buddy should the buddy then help with spelling or revisions in grammar. It's important to teach buddies how to use resources such as dictionaries, spellcheck, and other students to assist with editing, but only when the writer feels that the rest of the writing process is complete and the piece is done, except for cleanup. Whenever possible, especially with younger writers, I have the author hold the pencil so that it's the author making the editing changes suggested by the buddy. Writers should be in control of their own writing.

A Day in the Writing Workshop

Let me take you into a day in my writing workshop with a diverse group of eighth-grade language learners. I have found the following lesson to be an effective way to initiate writing workshop with students of a variety of ages and with language learners (including adults representing a variety of home languages). Since writers need to write about things they know, I focus on a unit I call "All about me" because it's a topic in which all writers have expertise. Even better, it's a topic that students of any age usually enjoy sharing with one another. The purpose is to help all writers find that they have ideas to write about and to get them started. I model ideas that I could write about and then elicit suggestions from the students. The key here is that whatever I model must be recognizable in the world of the students. This is not a time to model climbing Mount Rainier or piloting a small airplane, but it might be the time to model an experience I had with a dog, because most students have had an experience with a dog or with another animal. It's not the time to model spending winter vacation on the beaches of Hawaii, but it might be the time to model how the people I live with celebrate the winter holidays. We end up with topics like those in the following list, all constructed with the students with quick ten-second examples:

- Siblings or no siblings
- Time you were scared
- Vacations or times when there isn't school
- Family celebrations
- Friends or no friends
- Mischief
- First day of school
- Last day of school

- Celebrations
- Gifts
- What we do when school is out (vacations or weekends or afternoons)
- Cooking/food
- The first time I did something new
- Something that happened
- Funniest family stories

Broken up into the familiar format of the workshop, the day in this first writing workshop goes something like the following.

Connect/Purpose (What, Why, When)
(1–2 minutes)

Writers, I told you that we were going to have some regular time to write on Mondays, Wednesdays, and Fridays. We will have 45 minutes on each of these days because writers need regular time to write. Now, I could just say "start writing" and some of you would have ideas! But I bet many of you, like me and like many other writers, wouldn't have an idea. [What] *So today what I want to do is begin to share with you some ideas on how writers like us can get ideas to write about.* [Why] *And we're going to start with what we already know about—ourselves!* [When] *Starting with what we know can help us anytime we're writing. Let me show you what I mean.*

Model/Provide Information (How)

(3–5 minutes)

I knew that we would be writing today, so I started thinking about different things I knew about and might like to write about. Summer vacation just ended; that's an exciting time for my family because the relatives all gather at our house. It reminds me of Cynthia Rylant's book that we read yesterday, The Relatives Came, *except my relatives aren't quite as silly as those described in the book! But my Uncle Charlie, well, he IS a silly one! I have lots of stories I could tell about him, like the time he left hamburger on the counter and he also left our dog Bing in the kitchen! I think you can guess that we didn't have hamburgers for dinner that night.* Here I quickly sketch or model. *I wonder if you have relatives you might have stories about. Put your thumb up if you do. I see lots of thumbs up; I can't wait to read some of the stories about your relatives!* Pause.

As I was telling you about my relatives, I mentioned another character, my dog, Bing. He tries so hard to be good, but then he does something that's a bit naughty, and I can tell because he has a habit of smiling, really smiling, when he has done something. There was the time we found out he loved books as much as I do. I don't know if he thought he could read or what, but we came home and found three library books CHEWED UP! I hold up a library book and a picture of Bing and model chewing. *The strange thing was he chewed up ONLY the library books! How did he know which ones were the library books?! You can imagine that Mr. Buly wasn't very happy when he found out how much it cost to replace those! I wonder how many of you have pets or have known someone else's pet that did something a bit naughty. Or I wonder how many of you have had something destroyed by someone or something else, or perhaps you accidently broke something? Thumbs up if you did! Those are both things that I could write about today, but I could also write about something else. I know that we will be sharing stories with our families on Back-to-School Night, and I know I need to have a story done by then, so I'll want to get started today.*

Guided Practice

(2–3 minutes)

I shared some ideas with you about relatives, animals, and things getting broken or destroyed, and most of you had your thumb up at least once, reminding you of a story YOU had. Think about those for 15 seconds, and then I'm going to ask you to share the topic with your learning buddy. Don't tell too much, because he or she will want to read about it! Let's think. Pause for 15 seconds. ***Okay, partner B, please share with partner A.*** I have writing partners strategically paired, with the more verbal as partner B because the Bs usually have an idea to share and serve as another model for the A partners. I pause for another 15 seconds. ***Wow, I heard lots of exciting ideas! Now A, please share just the topic you are thinking about with your learning buddy.*** Pause for 15 seconds.

Link to Independent Work
(2–3 minutes)

Today, since it's the first day we've had writing workshop, you all have the opportunity to start a new piece of writing. If you know what you want to write about today, please put your thumb up. This assumes that I have previously held some whole-class lessons around our writer's notebook, conferencing, and the writing process. ***Fabulous; those of you with your thumb up, when I give the signal word, please move to your seats and get started. You'll have 30 minutes today, so you'll want to get started right away. Remember that I'll be checking in with you as you're writing today. I can't wait to hear about your stories.*** I use this arrangement so that those who don't yet have an idea or who are confused and need further support can stay with me and get the support they need to get started.

Independent Work
(30–60 minutes)

I start independent work by helping those who don't yet have a topic decide on one. I might need to model more topics, always modeling from things that I think are familiar in my students' lives. As each student decides on a topic, that student moves to his or her desk and begins to write. Today, my conferencing will simply consist of roaming the room and, if someone is not writing, checking in with a question. I'll ask something like ***What are you writing about today?*** If the student's answer suggests he or she still doesn't know what to write about, I'll hold a brief conference on getting an idea and check back with that student later in the workshop. As I conference, I also identify two or three students who might share what they have worked on or learned today. At least one of the modelers will be a language learner, so I make sure that student has an opportunity to rehearse with me. One of the modelers will be a student who really struggled to get started but found a topic. That's an important model for all my students. All of the students I identify to share will be sharing how they chose their topic today.

Sharing

(2–4 minutes)

Sharing begins with those students I've identified and talked with during conferences. This is important because I know that what these students share will reinforce today's teaching point—find a topic. I don't want to call on students randomly, because I won't know what they'll share. After the modelers share, I'll ask partners to take 20 seconds each to share with each other. This allows everyone to share during sharing time. This is a standard activity in my workshops; students know they'll each get a turn.

Close

(1–2 minutes)

I close the workshop by restating the teaching point and reminding the students when, where, and why they can use it. ***Writers, today and every day, when you are thinking of topics to write about, remember that one place to start is from all the things you already know about. Tomorrow we'll talk about some other ways to find topics.***

The Writing Conference

Like the reading workshop, the writing workshop format provides time for individual, small-group, or partner conferences. Conferencing is when you can differentiate instruction for specific students and specific writing tasks. All students, but language learners in particular, benefit from this one-on-one time with a teacher. Writing conferences provide so much information about what needs to be taught, even when students haven't written anything. When a student hasn't written anything, I need to find out why. It often means I need to hold a lesson with this student about getting started. As with the reading conference, the writing conference works best when students know what to expect. Both you and your students need to be familiar with the procedure. Before I begin writing conferences, I teach a procedural lesson that goes something like this:

Writers, we've spent the last few days learning about different ways that writers, like us, can get ideas for writing, and we've been getting some of our own ideas into our writer's notebooks. I see you all writing and I want to know more about the writing you're doing! So over the next few days, I will talk with each of you about your writing as we start writing conferences. This is what will happen.

I've made a Writers' Record of Learning notebook to use that has a page in it with each of your names. This is a place for me to keep notes about you as a writer, to help me know what to teach you. Once we've started our independent writing time today, I'm going to start making my way around the room. When I come to you, I'll ask something like this. I choose from the following questions and write two on the board. I usually start with the first two in almost every writing conference. Choose what feels right to you, or write your own questions.

How is it going?

What are you writing about?

Why did you decide to write about this?

What are you going to do next?

Is there anything I can help you with?

Let me show you what the conference is going to look like. Sally, would you bring the piece of writing you're working on and join me up here? I've already talked with Sally, so she knows I'm going to ask her to do this. I then model a conference with Sally and continue with my explanation. *It will take me a few days to conference with each of you, and I'll be conferring with you the rest of the year. It's the most important part of our learning time together, so it's really important that our learning time not be interrupted. If you need me while I'm conferencing, please put your name here on the whiteboard. I'll check in with you when I'm between conferences. Let me show you what this will look like.* I return to the model conference with Sally and have James start to come up but then move to the whiteboard to write his name. *Turn and talk to your partner. B's first; what will happen in a writing conference? A partners, what do you do if you need me? Any questions about what I'll be doing or you'll be doing during conferences? So today I'll be conferencing with you, getting to know you better as writers. I can't wait to talk with each of you!*

Writers' Record of Learning

I love teaching writing because the students and I have a product that we can examine together. I keep a spiral notebook with me when I'm conferring with writers. This is my Writers' Record of Learning, mentioned earlier in the chapter. Each page is headed by a single student's name. When I meet with a student, I note the date, what piece of writing the student is working on, where in the process the student is, and what we discussed. The discussion might include the writer setting a goal for what will happen before the next conference. I'll make a note of that goal so that I check in with the student again. The notes in my WRL might be things I want to teach this writer or things this writer wants to learn. Just as often, the notes will be about how a student has used something that has been taught or how the student has met a goal. Similar to the Readers' Record of Learning, the WRL is not kept secret from the student. I discuss what I write with the student and try to do the writing while I am still sitting with him or her.

The WRL informs my teaching, helps students set goals and self-assess their progress, and also serves as a formative assessment tool. It allows me to create and track a timeline of each student's progress as a writer. With WRL in hand, I can easily talk with parents, support specialists, or others about the progress a student is making. I can also look back at my instruction. If I'm teaching the same mini-lesson to different students, I know I need to move to a bigger group or whole-class lesson. If I'm revisiting the same teaching point again and again, I know I need to look at that teaching point and assess whether it's appropriate for my students' current development or determine how I can improve my instruction.

Summary

Writing workshop is especially beneficial for language learners because it provides teachers with time to meet each language learner where he or she is as a writer and move each student forward. The context of the workshop offers the support that language learners need to feel comfortable, allowing them to focus on the cognitive demands necessary to develop as writers.

A Time to Try . . .

1. Write a dialogue journal with one or two language learners. Simply write a letter inviting them to respond and begin to write back and forth. What do you find out about the students as individuals and as writers?

2. Refer back to Table 4.1. What additional lesson possibilities can you think of in each of the categories that would be appropriate for the students you currently teach? Incorporating state or district expectations can provide additional ideas.

3. Set up your own Writers' Record of Learning. Try a writing conference with one or two of your English language learners. What do the conferences suggest that each is ready to learn?

4. Take a look at your weekly schedule. Does each group of students get, at a minimum, three blocks of time for writing in a week? Are those blocks at least 45 minutes long? If not, what could you tweak in your schedule to allow for more of this critical writing time?

Some Favorite Resources

Anderson, C. (2000). *How's it going: A practical guide to conferring with student writers.* Portsmouth, NH: Heinemann.

Anderson, C. (2005). *Assessing writers.* Portsmouth, NH: Heinemann.

Anderson, J. (2005). *Mechanically inclined: Building grammar, usage, and style into writer's workshop.* Portland, ME: Stenhouse.

Calkins, L., et al. (2003). *Units of study for primary writing: A yearlong curriculum.* Portsmouth, NH: FirstHand.

Calkins, L., et al. (2006). *Units of study for teaching writing: Grades 3–5.* Portsmouth, NH: FirstHand.

Calkins, L., Hartman, A., & White, Z. (2005). *One to one: The art of conferring with young writers.* Portsmouth, NH: Heinemann.

Calkins, L. M. (1994). *The art of teaching writing.* Portsmouth, NH: Heinemann.

Ellis, L., & Marsh, J. (2007). *Getting started: The reading-writing workshop, grades 4–8.* Portmouth, NH: Heinemann.

Fletcher, R., & Portalupi, J. (2001). *Writing workshop: The essential guide.* Portsmouth, NH: Heinemann.

Fletcher, R., & Portalupi, J. (2007) *Craft lessons: Teaching writing K–8* (2nd ed.). Portland, ME: Stenhouse.

Samway, K. D. (2006). *When English language learners write: Connecting research to practice, K–8.* Portsmouth, NH: Heinemann.

Language Workshop and Considerations for Language Learners

Language acquisition does not require extensive use of conscious grammatical rules, and does not require tedious drill.

—STEPHEN KRASHEN (1981, PP. 6–7)

Twenty-four students are clustered in groups of four. Each group has a single sheet of paper with one of the following sentences on it: "Give a compliment about how the person is dressed"; "Ask for help on a school project"; "Disagree about a homework assignment." Under each sentence is a list of people: a principal, a parent, a grandmother, and a friend. The students have been charged with thinking about how they would address each of the people for the prompt given and writing their responses on a piece of chart paper. They are thinking of appropriate words to use to convey the same idea to different audiences. The room is abuzz with discussion, and it's not all in English, although all the writing the students are doing on the charts is in English. The students know they will be expected to share their phrases with the rest of the class using only English. Mrs. Paumier, the teacher, is moving around the groups checking in, guiding, and providing additional instruction as needed.

As in schools across the United States, the number of language learners is consistently increasing in the school where Mrs. Paumier teaches. Ten years ago, less than 5 percent of the school's population spoke languages other than English at home. In 2011, more than 35 percent of the students are language learners. In addition, as the socioeconomic level of the area has decreased, teachers have noted an increase in native English speakers who seem to have low language skills, similar to what Sheila Valencia and I (2004) found in our in-depth diagnostic work with students who didn't pass a fourth-grade state assessment. Through the 1980s, the school had continued to do what it had always done in terms of language development, and that was to focus on spelling. In the 1990s, the decade during which many of the teachers had completed teacher training, they learned that when students study isolated spelling lists, the new spelling doesn't transfer to writing. Students take a spelling test and promptly forget the words. So the school had settled on a spelling approach in which misspelled words were selected from students' writing, and each student worked individually on his or her own words. Even though they wrote a sentence using each word in a way that demonstrated understanding of the meaning of the word, students didn't seem to be gaining much in terms of either vocabulary comprehension or spelling. Teachers were concerned and didn't know what to try next. Although they had many years of teaching experience between them, they had little experience with language learners or students who came to them with low language skills. It was time to explore a new way of thinking about a spelling program and to add a language study component to the curriculum.

By that time, the school had successful reading and writing workshops operating in most classrooms. Teachers had based their original workshops on a combination of professional books and professional development, starting with Irene Fountas and Gay Su Pinnell's *Guiding Readers and Writers Grades 3–6: Teaching Comprehension, Genre, and Content Literacy* (2001). They had also been fortunate in their school district to have several years of professional development training through Margaret Mooney and R. C. Owen's Learning Network. Over the years, many of the teachers in Mrs. Paumier's school had become literacy coaches, focusing on reading and writing across grade levels. They had even moved the focus of reading and writing quite successfully into the content areas K–12, but they hadn't focused enough on language.

The move to add a language workshop to their already full day was gradual and began with an improvement in their approach to spelling, which they now called word study. *Words Their Way with English Learners: Word Study for Phonics, Vocabulary, and Spelling Instruction* (Bear, Helman, et al., 2007), written by a group of language scholars, started the teachers on their journey into word study and eventually into the language workshop. The first chapter of this book provided the teachers with a basic background in the English language, including a new understanding of how words had come into English. A few of the teachers became very excited about word study and began to implement a word study block in their classrooms, using *Words Their Way with English Learners* as their primary guide. This was a difficult transition, and they had to start slow. They began by teaching the procedures for word study to the whole class. Then they began to differentiate, first with two groups and eventually adding more groups as they could manage them. Although it made sense that students would be at different levels of word knowledge development, the teachers found it challenging to add differentiated word study groups to their already full schedule. But when they saw that spelling was improving for many of the students in classrooms using the word study block, they knew they were on their way to successful word study. They had found a way to focus on spelling and phonics that made sense to the students and to them. Still, the students' grammar was not improving and their vocabulary comprehension was still very low.

Looking back, the teachers who had started the word study groups realized that they had been drawing on the format they used for reading and writing workshop. They were focusing on one teaching point at a time, planning and teaching explicit mini-lessons, and moving students through a similar gradual release of responsibility process. Together, the teachers decided to emulate even more of the workshop approach during what they now called language workshop; however, they would devote just 15 to 20 minutes of their day to it. They replaced the time they had focused on spelling with the language workshop and reinforced the language teaching points throughout the day. Most of the teachers decided to devote two language workshops each week to spelling, two to language structure, and one to explicit vocabulary instruction, using the following format:

1 minute: connect

2 to 3 minutes: demonstration, modeling, or think-aloud

5 minutes: guided practice (engage) with link

10 to 13 minutes: exploration individually or in small groups

2 to 4 minutes: sharing back with the group

The teachers began by keeping Language Records of Learning (LRL) for their students, mimicking the notebooks they used for their reading and writing workshops. They kept one page for each student. On that page, they noted observations about a student's language structures, spelling, and vocabulary comprehension.

As they moved into the next year, the teachers across this and other districts realized that with the growing number of language learners in our K–8 classrooms, the language workshop is probably the most critical—and often overlooked—component of the literacy workshop. The teachers are finding that their intentional short lessons in the language workshop are helping them focus on what students need and then to reinforce those points and skills throughout the remainder of the day. Across K–8 schools, the teachers decided to dedicate a short amount of time each day to explicitly examine words and sentences, exploring how the English language works and adding breadth and depth to students' vocabulary knowledge. In the middle school, grades 6–8, where students have several teachers, the teachers decided to plan units of study for language workshop together in teams. That way, the teaching points explicitly taught in the language workshop can be reinforced throughout the day across various content areas.

The Components of Language Workshop

Grouping the elements of language study into three areas—language structures, vocabulary, and word study—helps me ensure that I am not focusing on one area while avoiding another. Some lessons or units of study, such as expanding vocabulary, the structure of English, use of pronouns, use of past tense, and the registers of English, will be equally pertinent to native English speakers and language learners, so many lessons will fit the needs of all your students and might be whole-class lessons. Other topics will be more specific to English language learners, such as similarities and differences between English and the home language. These lessons might be most effectively taught in small groups or during individual conferences. Table 5.1 lists sample mini-lessons selected because they are appropriate for many language learners, yet they are also important and effective for most learners in a classroom.

Tips for Teaching Language Structures

Understand That English Is Both Similar to and Different from Other Languages

Any linguistic system, or language system, is multidimensional. We use information about sentence structure to help us predict grammatical order and the form of words. But the language system of English may be different from that of other languages. In Spanish, for example, nouns normally precede adjectives. When reading in Spanish, we know what noun we are reading about before it is described. In English it is the opposite; adjectives normally precede the nouns they describe. To say "blue house" in Spanish, one says "*casa azul*" [house blue]. This is the type of structural information that is important for students to be explicitly taught, and students' misunderstandings provide us with clues about what they are ready to learn.

Language Structures	• Nouns follow adjectives in English (in Spanish it is the opposite). • *I go, you go,* but *he goes* (conjugations)
Vocabulary	• A focus on tier II words, the words that "travel well" across content domains (Beck, McKeown, & Kucan, 2002).
Word Study	• /Th/ often sounds and feels like /d/ but the tongue comes out of the mouth. • -ed endings

TABLE 5.1: Examples of Lessons in the Language Workshop

Recognize That Language Is Least Effectively Learned through Grammar Drills and Worksheets

Grammar drills do not help language acquisition and, in fact, can hinder both oral language and written language development. Such uncontextualized focus on language structure can raise the affective filter to a level that keeps students from taking risks. If we think about how children acquire their first language, this makes sense. Imagine a 5-year-old native English speaker running to the teacher to excitedly share that "I goed to the zoo!" Now imagine the child's response if the *teacher's* response is something like, *Joey, I'm glad you went to the zoo. Now, Joey, remember we've studied past tense. Go in the past tense is went. Let's conjugate that. Repeat after me, "I went, you went, he went, she went, we went, they went."* The native-English-speaking 5-year-olds I've worked with would have been much less likely to share with me if that were my response! And the feelings I would have left Joey with would have diminished, not enhanced, his language abilities. The same is true for language learners.

Restate Students' Statements with the Accepted Language Structure

Instead of correcting an incorrect language structure, use the correct structure in response. When Joey says, *I goed to the zoo,* your response could be, *Joey, you went to the zoo! I am so excited that you went to the zoo. I went to the zoo last year. We will go to the zoo later this year. What did you see?* If Joey had written this sentence in a dialogue journal, I would have written back with the same response, restating in a grammatically accurate manner what he had written, without commenting on his grammar.

The More Interaction with Native English Speakers through Reading, Writing, and Discussion, the Better

Our students begin the road through school with widely different knowledge, skills, and experiences with the English language. Some of our students have had wide exposure to books and conversations in English. Others have had great exposure, but in a language other than English. Still others may have had little exposure to book language or fewer opportunities for interactions with diverse groups of people. For most students, development of language structures comes through the experiences they have that enable them to engage in dialogue, read and hear many books, and have the opportunity to write for real purposes with feedback.

When students are isolated from the mainstream classroom to work on language structures, they lose native English speakers as models. The more integrated the language structure instruction can be with native English speakers, the stronger the language learners' development of English is likely to be.

Tips for Teaching Vocabulary

For language learners, the achievement gap, what some call the educational opportunity gap, is primarily a vocabulary gap (Carlo et al., 2004). The combination of different home languages, different proficiency in English, range of background experiences, and even the amount of books read at home are all related to the academic vocabulary students possess when they come to school. Knowledge of words and concepts begins long before a child walks

through the doors of the school and occurs in all the languages a child speaks. Bill Nagy (1988) writes, "Vocabulary knowledge is fundamental to reading comprehension; one cannot understand text without knowing what most of the words mean" (1). In the following sections, I share several tips from my work with language learners.

It's Possible for an English Language Learner to Bring 20,000 Words in a Home Language but Recognize Only 100 Words in English

Some first graders walk through the school doors with knowledge of about 5,000 words, whereas others arrive with 20,000 words (Moats, 2001). An English language learner might come to first grade with anywhere from 5,000 to 20,000 words in the home language but have very limited word recognition in English. For words that learners already know in one language, all they need are labels for those words or concepts in English; they don't need to be retaught word meanings or concepts. When there are language learners in the classroom, building vocabulary and adding labels, or the words we use for items and concepts, should be a focus of instruction throughout the day and across all content areas at any grade level. For example, if a student knows the word for *volcano* in Spanish, he or she simply needs the word, or label, we use in English. In classrooms of any grade level, using labels in English and in the languages of students can facilitate this relabeling while affirming home languages.

Vocabulary Knowledge Is More Than Simply Being Able to Say Words or Phonetically Identify a Word

Vocabulary knowledge includes understanding what words mean, including the multiple meanings that one word can have. For example, when I think of the word *field*, the first image that comes to mind is a big green baseball field. I know that a field is often a place where children play, but a field is also a place where farmers plant things. And *field* is used in science or even more generally to denote a particular area of study. A field can be specific to a sport—like that big green baseball field. I can also *field* a ball when playing baseball. A seemingly simple word like *field* actually has many layers or possibilities of meaning. All of those layers are critical to understanding the word and to being able to really "know" it.

Our goal for vocabulary instruction in the language block must be to help students develop deeper understandings of words. The more words we know the meaning of, and the more complexities of words we understand, the greater chance we have of understanding unknown text. In fact, a reader's general vocabulary knowledge is the single best predictor of how well a reader will understand text. Many students struggle as they progress through the grades due to the increasingly complex vocabulary. Not knowing the meaning of words limits not only reading but also writing, communicating orally, and understanding content instruction. One of our primary responsibilities is to provide opportunities for students to enlarge their vocabulary knowledge. If you've heard a word, you know what it sounds like, but if you know what the word *means,* as well as different meanings and uses for the word, then you *own* the word.

Remember that students can read fluently and understand what they are reading in English with a native language accent. It is easy to misinterpret a difference in pronunciation as a reading error, but these are very different miscues.

Some Vocabulary Does Not Need Explicit Instruction

Although we know that we learn most words *incidentally* through everyday experiences with oral and written language, including wide independent reading, research tells us that some vocabulary should be taught *explicitly,* especially to language learners. Choosing which words to focus on, however, can be a challenge. That's where the idea of tiers, described by Beck, McKeown, and Kucan (2002), has really helped me. They divide words into three tiers, or levels. Tier I words are basic words that rarely require instructional attention, even for English language learners: words such as *baby, clock, happy, walk, jump, hop, slide, girl, boy,* and *dog.* These are likely to be words or concepts that students know in another language; they simply need the labels in English. To teach these words, you can either provide a label or provide a word along with a picture or the actual object.

Skipping over tier II words for the moment, tier III words are low-frequency content words that students may not encounter again for years. These are the domain-specific words we find in our science or social studies units that might be important to understanding a particular concept but aren't words that students will encounter often in academic reading. Examples of tier III words are *photosynthesis, digestive,* and *alliteration.* These words require some attention when they are relevant to the content at hand, but often they are words that can be depicted pictorially, observed, or illustrated through an experiment or DVD. When I began teaching, I focused on tier III words from our social studies or science units for all of my students because I thought they were the essential words, those my bilingual learners most needed. I even added them to spelling lists as challenge words until I understood more about teaching vocabulary and word study.

Choose Tier II Words That "Travel Well" to Explicitly Teach

Tier II words and phrases are academic words used frequently in books and schools but not usually in daily conversation. These are the words we should focus on because they will come up again and again in a variety of academic domains. Tier II words are not exclusive to one event, one content, or one situation; they tend to cross over easily into a wide variety of settings and content areas, which is why they travel well. Beck and colleagues (2002) suggest that one way of identifying a tier II word is by recognizing that although you can explain it using tier I words, the tier II word provides a more specific definition. For example, a *hypothesis* is a "good guess"—*hypothesis*; or a *context* is a "setting"—*context*. For language learners, we need to include explicit instruction in tier II academic vocabulary like *hypothesis, context, illustrate*; signal words such as *therefore, even though, secondly*; and perhaps most confusing to language learners, idioms like "she broke my heart" or "give me a hand." These are the words and words within phrases that are powerful and travel well for language learners. Beck and colleagues suggest three concrete ideas to help you pick tier II words to teach: (1) words that are unfamiliar to students; (2) words that are critical to understanding passages of text; and (3) words that students are likely to encounter in the future.

Spending time defining, discussing, and clarifying vocabulary words necessary to meaning that are likely to be unfamiliar to the students before they read a passage is also important, as long as the words that are defined would not be clear in context. Because we acquire the majority of our vocabulary through wide reading, whenever words are supported by the context we should avoid explicitly defining them, instead letting students figure out meanings on their own, merely offering strategies during our language block to help them figure out words in context and checking in later.

"Brick" and "Mortar" Words and Phrases Provide More Ways to Think about What Needs to Be Taught

Dutro and Moran (2003) write about "brick" and "mortar" words to help us think about which words we need to teach. Brick and mortar words help to identify those that might fall into Beck et al.'s (2002) idea of tier II words because they are words that travel well and are essential to understanding. Although "mortar" words can be easily overlooked because they often seem so common, they can cause incredible confusion during reading. These words constitute the basic and general utility vocabulary required for constructing sentences. When we read or listen, mortar words determine relationships between and among other words, essentially holding our language together. I have also heard these referred to as "glue" words. Dutro and Moran (2003, pp. 239–40) offer the following categories of mortar words:

- **Connecting words:** *because, then, but, sometimes, before, therefore, however,* and *whereas*
- **Prepositions and prepositional phrases**: *on, in, under, behind, next to, in front of, between, among,* and *in the background*
- **Basic regular and irregular verbs**: *leave, live, eat, use, saw,* and *went*
- **Pronouns:** *she, he, his, their, it, each other,* and *themselves*
- **Academic vocabulary**: *notice, think, analyze, plan, compare, proof,* and *characteristics*

"Brick" words are those content and concept-specific words needed for a particular unit of study but that also travel well. Examples of brick words offered by Dutro and Moran (2003) include such words as *government, democracy, line, tone, metaphor, theme, variable, algorithm,* etc.

Thinking about which words are essential to teach from both a tier and a "bricks and mortar" perspective can greatly help us know what words will most help our students and are worth the time it takes to deeply learn.

Have Students Keep a Language Book

To help students keep track of the vocabulary and language structures they are learning and that they are interested in learning, try having them keep a language book. Students can use these books during explicit instruction to try new things or to write about what has been taught. They can also be books in which students keep words, phrases, and structures they have found interesting or confusing. When the word book includes a date for each addition, you have a way to assess the quality and quantity of words students are learning at various times. To construct language books, many sources suggest various modifications of Frayer, Fredrick, and Klausmeier's (1969) model; Figure 5.1 depicts the basic model. Notice the inclusion of examples and nonexamples as well as a drawing or picture. For language learners in particular, adding a picture that represents the word helps deepen understanding.

Tips for Teaching Word Study

Word study is a time for students to focus on how words work, including letters and their corresponding sounds and word identification skills such as being able to

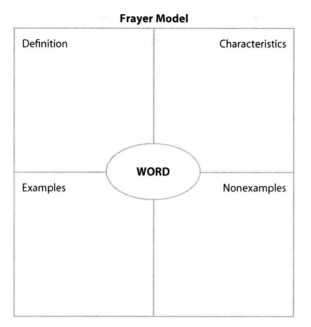

Frayer Model

| Definition | Characteristics |
| Examples | **WORD** | Nonexamples |

FIGURE 5.1: The basic Frayer model. (From D. A. Frayer, W. C. Fredrick, and H. J. Klausmeier. [1969]. *A Schema for Testing the Level of Concept Mastery* [Working Paper No. 16]. Madison, WI: Wisconsin Research and Development Center for Cognitive Learning.)

identify roots, prefixes, and suffixes; analogies; word patterns; and word families. Accurate spelling is also a part of word study. Word study ultimately leads to growth in vocabulary, and it becomes meaningful and enjoyable through active problem solving.

Decoding Does Not Equal Comprehension

Jim Cummins, an international expert on English language learners, writes that "[s]ystematic phonics instruction can enable second language learners to acquire word recognition and decoding skills in their second language to a relatively high level, despite the fact that their knowledge of the second language is still limited" (2003, p. 10). This quote has been used as a justification for explicit phonics instruction. However, Cummins follows with an additional sentence that is not always shared: "These decoding skills, however, do not automatically generalize to reading comprehension or other aspects of second language proficiency" (p. 10). My own learning of Spanish provides an example of the point Cummins makes. After living and teaching in Spain for three years, I can decode Spanish relatively well. But if you ask me what I've read, I might completely misunderstand something that I have accurately decoded. It's the same for English language learners; the ability to decode or pronounce words doesn't equal comprehension.

English Language Learners Will Likely Need Explicit Instruction in English Sounds Not Found in Their Home Languages

Phonemic awareness becomes important for language learners because of the differences between languages. These differences lead to the need for explicit instruction in sound–symbol relationships and the sounds, or phonemes, in English that differ from the other languages spoken, read, or written by language learners. I have found that the best way to decide where to focus attention on phonemic awareness is by examining the spelling of the language learners in my classroom. When language learners spell phonetically, they are demonstrating the sounds they already know and hear. Rather than considering any spelling "wrong," I first look to see what it is telling me about the confusions a language learner has between English and the home language. Table 5.2 provides examples of sounds found in English that are not found in other languages.

Analyzing How Students Spell Words Can Provide a Guesstimate of a Student's Current Word Knowledge and What Could Come Next

Analyzing students' writing or even isolated spelling, not for a grade but to inform instruction, can help you know what to teach. Donald Bear and his colleagues (Bear, Helman, et al., 2007; Bear, Invernizzi, et al., 2007) have created several diagnostic spelling inventories, available in any edition of *Words Their Way* and in multiple languages. The tool is given like a traditional spelling test, so it can be administered to a whole class at once, with the caveat that if students aren't sure how to spell a word, they should spell as much of the word as they can hear and "feel." To lower their affective filters (Krashen, 1994), you also need to reassure students that the inventory is not graded; it's used by teachers to help them teach. Once scored, the inventory

Spanish	consonant blends: st, sp, sk/sc, sm, sl, sn, sw, tw, qu (kw), scr, spr, str, squ vowels sounds: man, pen, tip, up; -r controlled vowels; schwa sound; caught, could, use Challenging final English sounds: rd, st, ng, sk, ng, z, oil, mp, dg
Chinese	b, ch, d, dg, g, oa, sh
Japanese	dg, f, l, th, th, oo, v, schwa
Greek	aw, ee, i, oo, schwa

TABLE 5.2: Examples of English Sounds Not Used in Other Languages. (Adapted from Fry, Kress, & Fountoukidis [2000] and Helman [2004].)

provides a guesstimate of each student's level of orthographic understanding. I have used the inventory with students and teachers from kindergarten through high school.

Inside the Language Workshop

Mrs. Gomez has a class of twenty-six energetic first graders, including a large group of bilingual learners; seventeen of the students are adding English, while nine speak English as the primary home language. Mrs. Gomez has carefully paired students into learning buddies. Knowing that student B is usually the stronger of the pair gives Mrs. Gomez a way to have the stronger student try something first. This helps her assess her mini-lesson instruction and decide when to move to practice, while often providing the less proficient student with an additional model.

Mrs. Gomez has noticed that many of her students are using but confusing past tense. Recognizing that this is a common instructional need for many students, both first and second language speakers of English, she has decided to focus a mini-lesson on tenses.

Connect/Purpose (What, Why, When)
(1–2 minutes)

Boys and girls, we've been talking about how to best share our ideas. That's something that is important all the time—making sure that what we say is understood. Yesterday, in our sharing time, I noticed that when you talked about what you're learning and what you've tried at home, you were talking about things that HAD happened. For example, today Halina was telling us about how she noticed a connection between a book her dad read to her and the book we read two days ago in class, and she was having a tough time figuring out how to talk about that particular day. She said "the yesterday before yesterday." I've noticed that lots of you struggle a bit when talking about things that happened two days ago. And the way we talk about the past is really important so that our listeners understand what we mean. [Why] I've especially noticed some

confusion about how we can talk about what happened two days ago. [What] We talk about what happened two days ago ALL the time—to our friends, to our family, in school. [When] So today what I want to show you is some ways you can talk about what happened two days ago.

Model/Provide Information (How)
(3–5 minutes)

Today is Friday. Mr. Lynch (the other first-grade teacher) wasn't here yesterday, so I didn't see him. But I wanted to tell him about what I did two nights ago. Mrs. Gomez shows on the class calendar that she is talking about two nights ago. I went to a concert and I heard the high school students sing—it was lovely. She shows a picture of the students singing. I wanted Mr. Lynch to know about it. So I said, "I went to a concert not yesterday, but the day that was before yesterday," and he gave me this funny look, like "What are you talking about?" and I thought—oh, that was confusing—I'd better try that another way, so I thought about what to say. I can say, "The day before yesterday." She writes this phrase on chart paper and will refer students back to it as they practice. Or I can say, "Two days ago." She adds to the chart paper. Or I could say the specific name of the day, "Wednesday." With each example, Mrs. Gomez uses the calendar to show the students how to go back to Wednesday. Wow, I have three ways that I can say this to Mr. Lynch that will not be confusing. I tried again: "Mr. Lynch," I said, "I went to a concert two days ago," and I looked at him to see if he was still confused, and he wasn't. "The concert was great! The high school students were singing." She shows the picture again of the high school students singing. "I hope you can go next time." She pauses. See how important it was for me to say this so that Mr. Lynch understood?

Two day ago it was Wednesday. Mrs. Gomez counts back on the calendar one and then two days. What happens in our classroom on Wednesdays? She has a chart of all the activities and events the class does on Wednesdays, with pictures or sketches next to each. We come to school; we go to music. She draws and writes each Wednesday activity or event on a new piece of chart paper, making a new list specific to that day. Two days ago, did anything else happen? Mrs. Gomez makes a list of four ideas and stops. She has decided that four is enough for one day. She makes sure that the phrases she writes will work with any of the starter phrases (Two days ago; Yesterday; The day before yesterday). On her list, generated by the students, are the following:

It was very windy.

It was indoor recess.

It was music day.

We played in the hall.

So if I was telling Mr. Lynch about this, I might say, "Two days ago it was very windy!" or I might say, "The day before yesterday it was very windy!"

Guided Practice
(2–3 minutes)

You get a chance to try this now with your language learning buddy. Partner A, you start first. Tell partner B about something you did two days ago. Start with "Two days ago." Mrs. Gomez points to the words *Two days ago* on the chart as she says the words. She pauses, listens, and checks for understanding. If she notices confusion, she will clarify or reteach at this point. She notices that her most beginning bilingual learner is quiet; she moves to the pair and models again. Everyone else seems to be doing well with this practice, so she decides to move on to a slightly more difficult practice. *Partner B, now it's your turn. Look at the other ways on our list to say "two days ago."* Mrs. Gomez points and says each starter. *Now it's your turn to choose one event and tell partner A something else that happened two days ago.* Mrs. Gomez pauses, listens, and checks for understanding. She notices a child who seems not to know what to do. She moves over and models for this pair. She then moves to another pair and models again. Notice that Mrs. Gomez started with partner A because she had modeled and provided a frame for the students— "two days ago." Then she had partner B try with a more difficult practice, selecting a different frame.

Sharing #1
(1–2 minutes)

Mrs. Gomez pulls the students back together and asks for someone to share what he or she *said* or *heard*. This gives Mrs. Gomez another way to check for understanding, for students to hear additional models, and for Mrs. Gomez to correct misunderstandings.

Link to Independent Work

Today and tonight when you're at home, listen for people talking about what happened two days ago, and tomorrow we'll have time to hear what you noticed! The link is for students to listen at home and report back—this pulls the lesson back to a real-life purpose rather than forcing artificial, context-removed practice in the classroom.

Sharing #2
(2–4 minutes)

Sharing happens again the next day and serves as a way to review and reinforce the previous day's lesson. As students share, Mrs. Gomez charts what they report, providing formative assessment data and material for additional mini-lessons on future days.

Close
(1–2 minutes)

Boys and girls, today, and every day, when you want to tell someone about something that happened two days ago, you have some words to use. I'm going to put the chart we've made on the wall. Mrs. Gomez posts the chart.

As in all workshops, the explicit lesson followed by practice is the key to learning. A language lesson in a K–2 classroom might sound quite different from a lesson in a 6–8 classroom, where more complex language structures are likely to be explored.

The Language Conference

The exciting aspect of helping students with language learning is that it is possible to observe individual needs during reading and writing conferences and then work with the whole class, small groups, or individuals during the language workshop or in conjunction with one of the other workshops.

Unlike with reading and writing conferences, I don't have a list of questions I ask during language conferences. My questions vary depending on what I have noticed about a student's use of language. If my conference is focusing on vocabulary, I might ask students if there are specific words or phrases they've heard that they are curious about. When I'm conferring to help a student examine a use of grammar, I already have the student's misunderstanding documented in my notes.

Students demonstrate their understandings of language throughout the day in their discussions with others, in their writing, and in their questions and responses in the classroom. As I listen to students throughout the day, I note what I hear or see in writing that suggests language confusion. I note what I hear and from whom on sticky notes and add them to my Language Record of Learning, on the appropriate student's page.

Humans seem to easily learn the language or languages they are born into and hear early; as they age, they have more difficulty hearing sounds in other languages that differ from the sounds of their home language. A conference common with language learners in my classrooms focuses on English pronunciation, usually a result of sound–symbol interference from the home language (see Kuhl, 2004). This conference often takes place during the language workshop, but it could also take place quickly during a reading or writing conference. When I notice Jose's improving pronunciation of English words and consider a next step, the conference might sound like this: ***Jose, it has only been a year since you have been learning English, and you are working so hard on your pronunciation! Earlier in the year, you worked on pronouncing each sound in a word in English—and now you are almost always hearing and feeling the difference when you pronounce /b/ for the letter b! Remember when you first came from Andalucía, you pronounced b as /v/? I'm going to make a note of that! I noticed that you're still working on the /th/ sound in English. That is a tricky sound, so different from the way it is often pronounced in Spanish—/d/. Watch me as I say the words the, this, these; what do you notice? Yes, my tongue comes out just a bit. That's the trick with /th/ in English; you can stick your tongue out at the teacher—but just a little! I'm going to make a note here to help me remember that you're working on this.***

Along with individual conferences, the LRL informs instruction for all students. In the mini-lesson that started this chapter, Mrs. Paumier consulted her LRL notebook, and the data confirmed what she thought she was noticing: 80 percent of her students, including most of the the English language learners, showed some confusion related to register. The majority tended to use either a register that was too formal with their classmates or that was too informal with the principal and other teachers. Because this was true for most of the students, and because proper register use is one of the state- and district-required objectives, Mrs. Paumier's explicit mini-lesson today, and her mini-language unit during her language workshop for the next few days, focused on the uses of different registers in English.

Summary

The language workshop is an especially critical part of the day for language learners. It provides a time to focus explicitly on vocabulary, language structures, and both similarities and differences between the language spoken in the classroom and the languages spoken in other settings. This includes differences between conversational and academic English as well as differences between languages. Explicit attention to language benefits all students, but especially language learners.

A Time to Try . . .

1. Keep a sticky note pad with or near you throughout the day, during all subjects. As (or immediately after) you are listening to students, especially language learners, talk with one another or you, make a quick note of any confused language structures you hear. What do your data suggest about appropriate instruction?

2. Pick a book that you would like to read to students in the next week. Read through the book, identifying three to five tier II words that you think will travel well, will be unknown to most of the language learners in your classroom, and are important to understanding the book. How can you introduce these words? Will sandwiching them with tier I words work? Are there other ways to model/demonstrate the meaning of the words?

3. Administer the diagnostic spelling inventory to your students. What differences in results do you notice between the language learners and the native English speakers in your classroom?

4. If possible, also administer the diagnostic spelling inventory in every student's home language and compare these results with those of the English spelling inventory. What more do you know after comparing the two?

Some Favorite Resources

Bear, D. R., Helman, L., Templeton, S., Invernizzi, M., & Johnston, F. (2007). *Words their way with English learners: Word study for phonics, vocabulary, and spelling instruction.* Upper Saddle River, NJ: Pearson.

Bear, D. R., Invernizzi, M., Templeton, S., & Johnston, F. (2007). *Words their way: Word study for phonics, vocabulary and spelling instruction* (4th ed.). Upper Saddle River, NJ: Pearson.

Beck, I. L., McKeown, M. G., & Kucan, L. (2002). *Bringing words to life: Robust vocabulary instruction.* New York: Guilford Press.

Freeman, D. E., & Freeman, Y. S. (2004). *Essential linguistics: What you need to know to teach reading, ESL, spelling, phonics, and grammar.* Portsmouth, NH: Heinemann.

Gibbons, P. (2002). *Scaffolding language, scaffolding learning: Teaching second language learners in the mainstream classroom.* Portsmouth, NH: Heinemann.

Common Questions
and Practical Answers

I n this final chapter, I address questions and leave you with a few tips for issues that come up frequently or that just didn't seem to fit into the previous chapters. If I don't address your question here, chances are good that others share your concern, and I would love to help you find resources and possible answers. Please feel free to contact me at Marsha.RiddleBuly@wwu.edu with additional questions, suggestions, or thoughts. We are most effective in reaching our language learners—and all our students—when we take the risk to ask one another questions and learn together.

Our school district uses a "pull-out" model for language learners; what can I do to still include my language learners in our classroom instruction?

Pull-out models continue to be widely used. The rationale is usually related to cost and efficiency; however, there is abundant research to suggest that pull-out models are the least effective means of language instruction. Thomas and Collier's (2002) research suggests that leaving students submerged in an English classroom, which is widely recognized as not very effective, is usually *more* effective for the students' language acquisition than implementing pull-out models. So the first thing to do is help others understand alternative ways of providing support to language learners.

Try inviting support teachers to work with the language learners within your class, where the support teacher will appropriately provide additional scaffolding to the students around what you are teaching. A side benefit is that while a teacher works with language learners, other students can also benefit from the additional support.

Many schools are exploring the use of English as a Second Language (ESL) or English Language Development (ELD) instructional coaches. An instructional coach is one who co-teaches or co-plans with the mainstream teacher, modeling best practices for language learners while supporting grade-level content in the mainstream classroom. It is imperative that an instructional coach not be perceived as an evaluator (Riddle Buly, Coskie, Robinson, & Egawa, 2004). Over the last ten years, many resources have been written to support instructional coaches (check out the Literacy Coaching Clearinghouse at http://www.literacycoachingonline.org /aboutus/literacy_coach.html).

Coordination between support teachers and mainstream teachers is always a challenge. In the best of scenarios, specialists are co-teaching and co-planning with the mainstream teachers. If co-teaching isn't an option, then coordinating a joint planning time with each teacher at least once a week can help students maintain grade-level content learning while developing language skills.

If bringing support staff into your classroom is not a possibility at this time, you must provide support teachers with the content objectives of your mainstream classroom. If the support teacher knows in advance what is being taught, he or she can embed the context and vocabulary of the topic in language support and other scaffolding so that students can cognitively focus on instructional content. That way, your students continue to get the content of the mainstream class, supported with appropriate language instruction, allowing them to be part of the mainstream classroom. Most important, if support teachers reinforce class content, students continue to make gains in grade-level content knowledge as they acquire English. When joint planning doesn't work, mainstream teachers can provide specialists with a preview of what is coming the following week. This still allows specialists to reinforce mainstream class content and objectives through language support.

If, as a teacher, I am able to speak the student's first language (such as Russian), how much should I translate for her? I know that it's good to make her feel comfortable, but I also don't want her always to wait for translation and not actually bother learning English.

Waiting for translation is exactly what a student will end up doing, either consciously or unconsciously, if a teacher is providing continual translation. This is not an effective way to help language learners acquire a new language. When is it okay to use the student's home language? If students seem confused about a concept, supporting their understanding in their home language can be helpful. Likewise, if an upcoming unit of study will introduce difficult English vocabulary, it might be a good idea for either you or a support teacher to preteach key vocabulary and concepts, using the students' first language to clarify when necessary. But during actual instruction, stick with English and use sheltering techniques to help students understand.

Remember, however, that it's always appropriate for students who speak the same home language to confer and clarify with one another in that language. As I discussed in Chapter 2, if you have experience traveling in another country whose language you don't speak, you'll understand how important it can be to have a chance to communicate with someone who speaks your own language. Clarifying with someone in a language you understand helps to both lower the affective filter and deepen understanding.

When trying to decide whether it's appropriate to use a student's home language, I ask myself what the objective of the lesson is—is it language learning or content learning? If I'm focusing on content, then using the student's home language is generally appropriate. If we're focusing on language instruction, speaking to the student in the home language probably isn't appropriate. The rule that works well for me is that students can talk with one another in whatever language they are most comfortable, but they must report out in English. This allows them to clarify concepts, definitions, or instructions using a home language but gives them practice in using the new language.

How can I embed language instruction into the reading and writing workshop?
Language instruction needs to be embedded throughout the day, not just in reading, writing, or language workshops. During instructional planning, you can identify potentially confusing language structures and vocabulary. You can also identify words for a quick word study or language structures to introduce or reinforce other studies. Even with the most thorough preplanning, however, words and structures will come up every day, across content areas, that you didn't anticipate. Being conscious of teachable moments and using techniques like sandwiching vocabulary, discussed in Chapter 2, throughout the day can be powerful for student learning. Here is another example of sandwiching vocabulary: If I use the word *infer* and it's a new term for my students, I sandwich the word by saying, "*Infer,* to make a good guess based on what we know and see, *infer.*" I've sandwiched the definition between the academic vocabulary word I'm using, providing the definition in words that I think are in the students' basic vocabulary.

When possible, link lesson topics or units of study across the literacy block to bring students to a deeper understanding of the topic of study. A unit on idioms, for example, can be powerful across the reading, language, and writing blocks, especially if you have many language learners in your room. Idioms can be introduced in the language block, independent books can be examined for idioms in the reading block, and common idioms can be introduced and practiced in the writing block.

What are some engaging reading materials for students?

The key to providing students with engaging reading materials is to have lots of different kinds of materials in a variety of genres at different reading levels available in all the languages spoken in your classroom, giving students plenty to choose from. Try letting students, both male and female, from your class and from older grades help you select books. They know what will interest their peers and other students of the age you teach. Allington and colleague (Allington & McGill-Franzen, 2003; McGill-Franzen & Allington, 2003) found that books about current pop culture icons—e.g., teen actresses and actors, athletes—were the most popular of all the books available in summer reading programs. Dav Pilkey's Captain Underpants series was included in the top choices. Some of us cringe at the students' choices of books, but then they would cringe at many of our choices! Just like us, students need to read materials they enjoy, and what they enjoy may be quite different from what we think they should read or will enjoy. Allington and McGill-Franzen note that to appeal to both boys and girls of different ages it's important to include books and magazines about topics such as cars, mechanics, and video games as well as series books like the Diary of a Wimpy Kid books by Jeff Kinney.

For early beginning English readers, Suzy Rau, a district ELL coordinator and a trained Reading Recovery teacher, has some favorite resources she uses for independent reading, take-home reading, guided instruction, and tutoring:

Pioneer Valley Books by Michelle Dufresne: http://www.pioneer valleybooks.com/spanish.html

MaryRuth Books by Mia Coulton: http://www.maryruthbooks.com

Reading Reading Books by Kris Bonnell: http://www.readingreading books.com/

These three resources all exhibit characteristics recommended by Reading Recovery, including recurring characters as the challenge of the books increases, color photographs, and stories with familiar subjects that are relevant to young readers. In addition, the pictures and illustrations support the text and encourage the reader to focus on words and story.

Suzy's description of why these books support language learners fits with Cummins's (1994) quadrant of language acquisition: if we can use what we already know about characters, settings, and typical things that happen within a series, we have more cognitive energy to put toward new language and new content ideas. Richard Allington (2011) tells us that reading texts with the same characters or settings supports readers because they already know the personalities of the characters and have some schema as they progress through series books that become gradually more challenging. The key to choosing books is to remember that there is no one "right" list of books or materials. The right books and materials must be those that engage and support your particular students, even if those texts don't engage you.

If we expect students to learn English, doesn't it make sense for them to use only English at home?

This is one of the great fallacies of language learning. Encourage parents and students to speak the strongest language of the family at home. It is through this rich oral interaction that vocabulary and concepts develop. Once we've learned the meaning of a word in one language, all we need is a new label for that word in the second language (or third or fourth). A sixth-grade boy recently referred to me had moved from Mexico to the United States in third grade but still spoke only Spanish. His previous teachers, with the best of intentions, had told the boy's mother to speak only English at home. But the mother was an English language learner herself; while her Spanish was rich, her English was limited. The result was a sixth-grade student who lacked deep literacy in both English and Spanish.

This student would have benefited more from speaking with his mother in Spanish at home and having her read to him in Spanish. Many strategies and skills transfer from one language to another. If they're not learned deeply in any language, the student ends up semi-literate—unable to read, write, or speak fluently—in both the home language and the language of school, and we have greatly exacerbated the student's normal learning struggles. See Chapter 2 for more on this, along with the research to support it.

Should I assess my language learners as I do all my other students?
This is such a common and difficult question. Part of the answer depends on what your school and district expect on report cards. In a standards-based society such as ours, it is only fair to let students and their parents know where the students stand in terms of state and now federal standards.

However, it's also important to recognize the difference between language challenges and content challenges. A student might understand most social studies, science, and math concepts but not be able to explain that understanding in English on a traditional test. When possible, include alternative methods for students to demonstrate understanding. For example, to show sequence in writing, students could draw a plan and then write in their home language. To show comprehension in science or social studies, students could use art, drama, or home language to show their understanding. If a language learner can't demonstrate understanding in English, don't assume the language learner doesn't understand the concept.

How can I tell if a student really doesn't understand my instruction, or if the student is using the language barrier as a way to get out of work (i.e., do the students actually understand more than they let on)?
Wondering whether students are confused by a concept or confused by language requires us to look at their understanding apart from language. Refer back to the Cummins's quadrant in Chapter 2 (Figure 2.1) and consider your instruction. Has instruction been appropriately sheltered? Can you add pictures or objects? Can you add additional modeling or demonstration? Is there another speaker of a student's home language available who can help you find out more? Is there another way to assess the student's understanding? Can the student draw or perform or show you his or her understanding in a way that doesn't require language?

Is it better to communicate with parents in English or in their native language in written communication?
Some bilingual teachers say that it's better to translate if you can to ensure clear understanding, while others claim you should send everything home in English because it forces parents to seek out help and learn English themselves. However, the purpose of communicating with parents is for parents to understand the messages you are sending about their children, not to teach parents English. Communicating in the language in which parents have the greatest written proficiency is best. If you want to support

parents' acquisition of English, provide them with resources for language classes or offer such classes yourself.

Should I encourage families to speak only English at home?
Again, parents should be encouraged to speak with and read to their children in their strongest language(s). Too often the well-intentioned but misinformed suggestion of speaking, reading, and writing only in English has been drilled into emerging bilingual parents. Parents who may be fully fluent in their home language find themselves attempting to converse in English, with a limited vocabulary in English. This doesn't help their children develop language and vocabulary knowledge.

How can I encourage parents who don't speak English to get involved in their child's school activities?
Most parents want to be involved in their children's education. Depending on the culture the parents come from, the extent to which classroom involvement has been encouraged can differ dramatically. For example, educators I've worked with in both the United States and Mexico have told me that in Mexico parents are rarely encouraged to assist in classrooms. Therefore, the first step is to make sure parents know you *want* them to be engaged.

It's also important to have someone at the school who can communicate in the home language of the parents whenever possible. This doesn't have to be the classroom teacher; it might be another parent or an instructional assistant who speaks both English and the home language. Some schools have bilingual instructional assistants available at a certain hour of the day (or once a week) who can talk with parents or guardians. Other schools support family liaisons who are responsible for going out into the community to provide information and invitations to families. Other schools hold monthly ELL information meetings, with translators for each language represented. Translators contact parents in advance to find out who will be attending so that translators are ready and waiting. In these meetings, they go over news that has been sent to parents in English, discuss upcoming events, and together fill out forms that would be difficult or impossible for parents to fill out in English on their own.

One of the most exciting ways to engage parents is through family-oriented events like literacy nights. During a literacy night, families come together at the school to create something that tells a family story; this something might be a single-language book, a bilingual book, a drawing, a skit, a song. This get-together provides an engaging way to include families while also providing a rich means for students and the teacher to get to know one another better.

Another way to engage parents is to find out what they would like to know more about and then arrange workshops. These might be English as a Second Language courses, a discussion held in different home languages about the required math curriculum, or perhaps an exploration held in the language of the families of home strategies that families can use to support their children's schoolwork. We did this recently in one community and found that the parents had many questions about how to support home-work at home. We were able to provide that information in the languages of the parents. Being willing to reach out to families is key to good school–parent relationships.

Without drawing too much attention to the language learners in the class who are experimenting with English, how can a teacher foster a level of understanding among the other students in the class?

We all have different strengths and needs—all of us. The classroom is a place where we can all be learners with different strengths, where we help one another, and where it's safe to take risks. It's easier, of course, to write this than to create this kind of classroom, but it is imperative. The time you spend on creating a classroom community is time well spent. Chapter 2 provides ideas and resources for creating a comfortable and safe classroom of learners.

What are some resources for building my materials in the various home languages of my students?

There are many materi-als available for purchase and more appear each day. Doing a simple Internet search using as key words a specific language (say, "Spanish") and "educa-tion" will bring up many resources. Attending state or regional associations for bilingual education is a way to review materials available from different educational publishers; the National Association for Bilingual Education (NABE) at www.nabe.org has links to state and regional associations. Contacting members of state organizations and asking for favorite resources in a particular language is another way to locate materials. Some countries publish educational materials themselves. For example, Mexico has a National Reading Program and has made copies of the materials available to schools in the United States.

One of the least expensive sources of materials comes from our own classrooms—older students in our schools, families, and community members. High school students can translate materials they are studying in science or social studies into their home languages (with a fully proficient language user checking the final editing), and community members can dictate stories or cultural norms to proficient writers of the language. Community college and university language courses provide another means for the creation of materials; class books and class-made materials provide yet another. And of course there is the Internet. In every case, however, you need to have a proficient reader of the language vet the materials, screening for bias and appropriate content and doing a final edit. Some school districts set up bias and review committees for such a purpose. Community organizations and churches are a good source of proficient users of home languages who can assist with locating, screening, or developing appropriate materials.

Does the format of the literacy workshop always follow the same pattern?
The format of the workshop does change to suit the individual teacher or the content as teachers become familiar with it. I have found that teachers who feel the most comfortable using the workshop, and who implement it effectively, stick with the format I've presented here (see Figure 6.1) until they have a good reason for making modifications. Regardless, the content of each element of the workshop remains the same, and the critical connections for students of what, why, when, and how are always included. There may be times, however, when you realize that you don't need a guided practice. Or you may be able to go straight to a demonstration with a small group or one-on-one with a student.

What does a week look like with reading, writing, and language workshops?
The way a teacher structures a week is dependent on the school, the amount of time available for workshops, specials, and partner teachers. The schedule in Figure 6.2, however, is one way to intentionally incorporate reading, writing, and language each day.

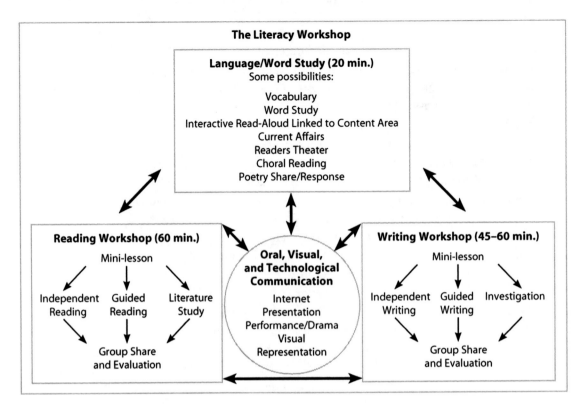

FIGURE 6.1: Basics of the literacy workshop.

15 minutes: Morning meeting, morning message, word of the day, and read to (content area or literary element focus; vocabulary, language, text structure, oral language)

10 minutes: Large-group writing lesson (connect/demonstration/model)

30 minutes: Writing workshop (independent writing, teacher roves in and out with 1-to-1 writing conferences; when able to manage, move to flexible guided writing groups based on the changing needs of students)

5 minutes: Sharing from writing, refocus

20 minutes: Language block (spelling, phonics, and vocabulary)

15 minutes: Large-group reading lesson (connect/demonstration/model)

20 minutes: Independent reading and/or literature circles for majority of students, teacher either 1-to-1 conferences or needs-based guided reading groups

5 minutes: Teacher roves, managing, answering individual questions, helping students get on track, 1-to-1 conferences

20 minutes: Independent reading and/or literature circles for majority of students, teacher either 1-to-1 conferences or needs-based guided reading groups

15 minutes: Debrief/lessons learned

(Example questions: What did you learn about inferring today? What did you learn about revision today? What questions do you have? Students share examples that the teacher has identified during workshop time.)

15 minutes: Read to with vocabulary attention (content area reading)

FIGURE 6.2: Literacy block minutes per day for reading, writing, and language workshops.

One of the most complex structures I've worked with was in a dual language school, where two groups of students switched between two teachers throughout the school day. What follows are the schedules we drafted for K–2 (Table 6.1) and 3–5 (Table 6.2). I offer these schedules as examples, hoping that the complexity of these schedules offers simplicity for those instituting less complicated structures. In this particular dual language school, students receive instruction in reading and writing in their home language for only an hour and half each day through second grade. Starting with grade 3, students receive reading and writing instruction in both Spanish and English each day. Language is a focus throughout the day in all content areas. The interactive read-alouds in content area studies are a time when the teacher can link the strategies and skills taught authentically to instructional content.

Time	Spanish Teacher	English Teacher
8:30 – students go to homeroom	Dialogue journals	Dialogue journals
9:00–10:30	Spanish literacy	English literacy
9:00–9:45	Writing workshop M/T/W/Th	Writing workshop M/T/W/Th
	Language workshop Th/F	Language workshop Th/F
9:45–10:30	Reading workshop M/T/W/F	Reading workshop M/T/W/F
10:30–10:45	Recess	Recess
10:45–12:00	Social studies/science Group 1 Interactive read-aloud (content based)	Math Group 2 Interactive read-aloud (content based)
12:00–12:45	Lunch	Lunch
12:45–2:00	Social studies/science Group 2 Interactive read-aloud (content based)	Math Group 1 Interactive read-aloud (content based)
2:00–2:25	Specials or homeroom or centers or . . . (homeroom swaps at half-year)	Specials or homeroom or centers or . . . (homeroom swaps at half-year)
2:25	Home	Home

TABLE 6.1: Example of a K–2 Dual Language Schedule

Time	Spanish Teacher	English Teacher
8:30–9:00	Students arrive, free reading in language of choice (builds vocabulary)	Students arrive, free reading in language of choice (builds vocabulary)
9:00–10:30	Spanish literacy and social studies/science and interactive read-aloud (content based) Group 1 M/T/W Reading workshop 9:00–10:30 Th/F Writing workshop 9:00–10:30 M/T/W Language workshop 10:30–10:45	English literacy and math and interactive read-aloud (content based) Group 2 M/T/W Writing workshop 9:00–10:30 Th/F Reading workshop 9:00–10:30 Th/F Language workshop 10:30–10:45
10:30–10:45	Recess	Recess
10:45–11:45	Continue Spanish literacy and social studies/science and interactive read-aloud (content based) Group 1	Continue English literacy and math and interactive read-aloud (content based) Group 2
11:45	SWITCH	SWITCH
	Interactive read-aloud Group 2 (content based)	Interactive read-aloud Group 1 (content based)
12:20–12:45	Lunch	Lunch
12:45–3:00	Spanish literacy and social studies/science and interactive read-aloud (content based) Group 1 M/T/W Reading workshop 9:00–10:00 Th/F Writing workshop 9:00–10:15 M/T/W Language workshop 10:00–10:45	English literacy and math and interactive read-aloud (content based) Group 1 M/T/W Writing workshop Th/F Reading workshop Th/F Language workshop
3:00	Specials (or built into the day)	Specials (or built into the day)

TABLE 6.2: Example of a Grades 3–6 Dual Language Schedule

GRADES 3–6

In grades 3-6 in this dual language school, students receive literacy instruction in both Spanish and English each day. Writing workshop and reading workshop are alternated across these languages, and strategies and skills are integrated with social studies, science, and math content when possible. Notice in Table 6.2 the 15-minute language block each day in both languages. Students also have reading workshop and writing workshop each day, but usually in only one language. Although students need time to read and write daily, it doesn't have to be in both languages. Teachers modify times throughout the year to keep the literacy instruction time in both languages approximately equal. Whenever possible, they work on the same units of study for reading and writing but instruct in different languages.

Michelle Hornof, an amazing fifth-grade teacher with many language learners in her classroom, is using the schedule in the following chart this year. Michelle calls her language block "word study" but basically incorporates the same areas described for the language workshop in Chapter 5.

Monday	Tuesday	Wednesday	Thursday	Friday
Strings Morning Meeting	9:05–9:50 PE	9:05–9:50 PE	9:05–9:35 Music	9:05–9:50 PE
Science/SS 10:25–10:45 Word Study	9:50–10:25 Music Morning Meeting	9:50–10:35 Library Morning Meeting	Morning Meeting 9:45–10:45 Science/SS	Morning Meeting 10–10:45 Science/SS
Snack/Morning Recess 10:45–11:00				
Math	Word Study	Word Study	Word Study	Word Study
	Math	Math	Math	Math
Pack up/Lunch/Recess 12:15–1:05				
1:05–1:25 Read-Aloud	1:05–1:25 Read-Aloud	1:05–1:25 Read-Aloud	1:05–1:25 Read-Aloud	1:05–1:25 Read-Aloud
1:25–2:25 Reading Workshop	1:25–2:25 Reading Workshop	1:25–2:25 Reading Workshop	1:25–2:25 Reading Workshop	1:25–2:25 Reading Workshop
2:25–3:25 Writing Workshop	2:25–3:25 Writing Workshop	2:25–3:25 Writing Workshop	2:25–3:25 Writing Workshop	2:25–3:25 Writing Workshop

GRADES 6–8

Often, middle school language arts courses are about 50 minutes long. That's just too short. Combining a 50-minute language arts course with a 50-minute content course allows time for richer instruction and practice in reading, writing, and language. If all you have is 50 minutes, however, you might try the following time configurations:

M/W/F

5 minutes: language study

10 minutes: writing lesson

30 minutes: independent writing

5 minutes: share

T/Th

5 minutes: language study

10 minutes: reading lesson (includes language discussion)

30 minutes: independent reading

2 minutes: share

What are some simple daily tips to keep in mind?

Drawing from various sources, Bracken Reed and Jennifer Railsback (2003) compiled and adapted a list of ten ideas for mainstream teachers of English language learners. These ten tips, slightly adapted again, can be used within the workshop to help you provide explicit differentiated instruction in a risk-free environment.

1. Enunciate clearly, but do not raise your voice. Add gestures, point directly to objects, or draw pictures when appropriate.

2. Write clearly, legibly, and in print; many ELL students have difficulty reading cursive.

3. Develop and maintain routines. Use clear and consistent signals for classroom instruction.

4. Repeat information and review frequently. If a student does not understand, try rephrasing in shorter sentences and simpler syntax. Check often for understanding, but do not ask, "Do you

understand?" Instead, have students demonstrate their learning to show comprehension.

5. Try to avoid idioms and slang words unless you explicitly include a definition.

6. Present new information in the context of known information.

7. Announce the lesson's objectives and activities, and list instructions step by step.

8. Present information in a variety of ways.

9. Provide frequent summations of the salient points of a lesson, and always emphasize key vocabulary words.

10. Recognize student success overtly and frequently. But also be aware that in some cultures, overt, individual praise is considered inappropriate and can therefore be embarrassing or confusing to the student.

Summary

As the number of language learners increases in mainstream classrooms, we will undoubtedly continue to have questions about the most effective ways to meet not only their needs but also the needs of all our students. The most effective teachers I know tend to be those who continually risk asking questions and who discuss possible solutions with other educators. Just as our students learn best together, so do educators. This chapter provided brief responses to several commonly voiced questions about teaching, reaching, and engaging English language learners in literacy workshops. These questions and responses will no doubt bring more questions and ideas as together we continue to learn how to effectively engage and teach the increasingly diverse students we are fortunate enough to have in our classrooms.

A Time to Try . . .

1. Write out your current weekly schedule. How can you tweak the times so that you have at least three days of writing instruction, five days of reading instruction, and a short language study each day? Can any of the reading, writing, or language be combined with other content studies?

2. What additional questions do you have? If you are reading with a group, list your additional questions and divvy up the work of researching and suggesting answers!

Some Favorite Resources

My favorite resource is talking with teachers from various schools and grade levels. These day-to-day "experts" have discovered or devised a variety of practice-proven means of reaching and teaching their language learners.

Cary, S. (2007). *Working with English language learners: Answers to teachers' top ten questions* (2nd ed.). Portsmouth, NH: Heinemann.

Crawford, J., & Krashen, S. (2007). *English learners in American classrooms: 101 questions, 101 answers.* New York: Scholastic.

Freeman, Y. S., Freeman, D. E., & Ramírez, R. (Eds.). (2008). *Diverse learners in the mainstream classroom: Strategies for supporting ALL students across content areas—English language learners, students with disabilities, gifted/talented students.* Portsmouth, NH: Heinemann.

Works Cited

Allington, R. (2011, March). *Is RTI our last, best hope for the future of reading?* Keynote Presentation at the Urgency and School Change Conference, Seattle, WA.

Allington, R., & McGill-Franzen, A. (2003, November). Use students' summer-setback months to raise minority achievement. *Education Digest, 69*(3), 19–24.

Almasi, J. F. (2003). *Teaching strategic processes in reading.* New York: Guilford Press.

Arnold, T. (1997). *Parts.* New York: Dial.

Arnold, T. (2001). *More parts.* New York: Dial.

Arnold, T. (2004). *Even more parts.* New York: Dial.

August, D., & Hakuta, K. (Eds.). (1998). *Educating language-minority children.* Washington, DC: National Academy Press.

Bear, D. R., Helman, L., Templeton, S., Invernizzi, M., & Johnston, F. (2007). *Words their way with English learners: Word study for phonics, vocabulary, and spelling instruction.* Upper Saddle River, NJ: Pearson.

Bear, D. R., Invernizzi, M., Templeton, S., & Johnston, F. (2007). *Words their way: Word study for phonics, vocabulary and spelling instruction* (4th ed.). Upper Saddle River, NJ: Pearson.

Beck, I. L., McKeown, M. G., & Kucan, L. (2002). *Bringing words to life: Robust vocabulary instruction.* New York: Guilford Press.

Bialystok, E., Craik, F. I. M., & Freedman, M. (2007). Bilingualism as a protection against the onset of symptoms of dementia. *Neuropsychologia, 45,* 459–464.

Bialystok, E., & Peets, K. F. (2010). Bilingualism and cognitive linkages: Learning to read in different languages. In M. Shatz & L. C. Wilkinson (Eds.), *The education of English language learners: Research to practice* (pp. 133–151). New York: Guilford Press.

Boushey, G., & Moser, J. (2006). *The daily five: Fostering literacy independence in the elementary grades.* Portland, ME: Stenhouse.

Boushey, G., & Moser, J. (2007). *The daily five alive! Strategies for literacy independence* [DVD]. Portland, ME: Stenhouse.

Braiman, J. (2010). *Literary devices.* Retrieved from http://www.oshkosh.k12.wi.us/faculty_pages/kromholz/Terminology.cfm

Brechtal, M. (2001). *Bringing it all together: Language and literacy in the multilingual classroom* (rev. ed.). Dominie Press.

Calkins, L., et al. (2003). *Units of study for primary writing: A yearlong curriculum.* Portsmouth, NH: FirstHand.

Calkins, L., et al. (2006). *Units of study for teaching writing: Grades 3–5.* Portsmouth, NH: FirstHand.

Calkins, L., Tolan, K., Ehrenworth, M., Khan, H. A., & Mooney, J. (2010). *Units of study for teaching reading, grades 3–5: A curriculum for the reading workshop.* Portsmouth, NH: Heinemann.

Calkins, L. M. (1994). *The art of teaching writing.* Portsmouth, NH: Heinemann.

Cappellini, M. (2005). *Balancing reading and language learning: A resource for teaching English language learners, K–5.* Portland, ME: Stenhouse.

Carlo, M. S., August, D., McLaughlin, B., Snow, C. E., Dressler, C., Lippman, D. N., Lively, T. J., & White, C. E. (2004). Closing the gap: Addressing the vocabulary needs of English-language learners in bilingual and mainstream classrooms. *Reading Research Quarterly, 39,* 188–215.

Chamot, A. U., & O'Malley, J. M. (1996). The Cognitive Academic Language Learning Approach: A model for linguistically diverse classrooms. *Elementary School Journal, 96*(3), 259–273.

Clay, M. M. (1993). *Reading recovery: A guidebook for teachers in training.* Portsmouth, NH: Heinemann.

Cloud, N., Genesee, F., & Hamayan, E. (2009). *Literacy instruction for English language learners: A teacher's guide to research-based strategies.* Portsmouth, NH: Heinemann.

Coskie, T. L. (2009). Building in authenticity. *School Talk, 14*(3), 1–2.

Cummins, J. (1979). Cognitive/academic language proficiency, linguistic interdependence, the optimum age question and some other matters. *Working Papers on Bilingualism, 19,* 121–129.

Cummins, J. (1981). The role of primary language development in promoting educational success for language minority students. In California State Department of Education (Ed.), *Schooling and language minority students: A theoretical framework* (pp. 3–49). Los Angeles: Evaluation, Dissemination and Assessment Center, California State University.

Cummins, J. (1994). Primary language instruction and the education of language minority students. In C. F. Leyba (Ed.), *Schooling and language minority students: A theoretical framework* (2nd ed., pp. 3–46). Los Angeles: Evaluation, Dissemination and Assessment Center, California State University.

Cummins, J. (2001). *The academic and political discourse of minority language education: Claims and counter-claims about reading, academic language, pedagogy, and assessment as they relate to bilingual children's educational development.* Summary of paper presented at the International Conference on Bilingualism, Bristol, England, April 20, 2001. Retrieved from http://iteachilearn.org/cummins/claims.html

Dole, J. A. (2000). Explicit and implicit instruction in comprehension. In B. M. Taylor, M. F. Graves, & P. van den Broek (Eds.), *Reading for meaning: Fostering comprehension in the middle grades* (pp. 52–69). Newark, DE: International Reading Association.

Duffy, G. G., Roehler, L. R., Meloth, M. S., Vavrus, L. G., Book, C., Putnam, J., & Wesselman, R. (1986). The relationship between explicit verbal explanations during reading skill instruction and student awareness and achievement: A story of reading teacher effects. *Reading Research Quarterly, 21,* 237–252.

Duke, N. K., Purcell-Gates, V., Hall, L. A., & Tower, C. (2006). Authentic literacy activities for developing comprehension and writing. *Reading Teacher, 60,* 344–355.

Durkin, D. (1978–1979). What classroom observations reveal about reading comprehension instruction. *Reading Research Quarterly, 14,* 481–533.

Dutro, S., & Moran, C. (2003). Rethinking English language instruction: An architectural approach. In G. G. García (Ed.), *English learners: Reaching the highest level of English literacy* (pp. 227–258). Newark, DE: International Reading Association.

Echevarría, J., Vogt, M., & Short, D. J. (2008). *Making content comprehensible for English learners: The SIOP model* (3rd ed.). Boston: Pearson/Allyn and Bacon.

Filipović, Z. (1994). *Zlata's diary: A child's life in Sarajevo.* New York: Scholastic.

Finch, M., & Beath, M. (1993). *The A, B, C of the biosphere.* Oracle, AZ: Biosphere Press.

Fisher, D., Rothenberg, C., & Frey, N. (2007). *Language learners in the English classroom.* Urbana, IL: National Council of Teachers of English.

Fitzgerald, J. (1993). Literacy and students who are learning English as a second language. *Reading Teacher, 46,* 638–647.

Fletcher, R. (1992). *What a writer needs.* Portsmouth, NH: Heinemann.

Fletcher, R. (2011). *Mentor author, mentor texts: Short texts, craft notes, and practical classroom uses.* Portsmouth, NH: Heinemann.

Fletcher, R., & Portalupi, J. (2001). *Writing workshop: The essential guide.* Portsmouth, NH: Heinemann.

Fletcher, R., & Portalupi, J. (2007). *Craft lessons: Teaching writing K–8* (2nd ed.). Portland, ME: Stenhouse.

Fountas, I. C., & Pinnell, G. S. (1996). *Guided reading: Good first teaching for all children.* Portsmouth, NH: Heinemann.

Fountas, I. C., & Pinnell, G. S. (2001). *Guiding readers and writers grades 3–6: Teaching comprehension, genre, and content literacy.* Portsmouth, NH: Heinemann.

Frayer, D. A., Fredrick, W. C., & Klausmeier, H. J. (1969). *A schema for testing the level of concept mastery* (Working Paper No. 16). Madison: Wisconsin Research and Development Center for Cognitive Learning.

Freeman, Y., & Freeman, D. (2004*).* Connecting students to culturally relevant texts. *Talking Points, 15*(2), 7–11.

Freeman, Y. S., & Freeman, D. E. (2009). *Academic language for English language learners and struggling readers: How to help students succeed across content areas.* Portsmouth, NH: Heinemann.

Fry, E. B., Kress, J. E., & Fountoukidis, D. L. (Eds.). (2000). *The reading teacher's book of lists* (4th ed.). San Francisco: Jossey-Bass.

Gibbons, P. (1991). *Learning to learn in a second language.* Newtown, NSW, Australia: Primary English Teaching Association.

Gibbons, P. (2002). *Scaffolding language, scaffolding learning: Teaching second language learners in the mainstream classroom*. Portsmouth, NH: Heinemann.

González, N., Moll, L. C., & Amanti, C. (Eds.). (2005). *Funds of knowledge: Theorizing practices in households, communities, and classrooms*. Mahwah, NJ: Erlbaum.

Harvey, S. (1998). *Nonfiction matters: Reading, writing, and research in grades 3–8*. Portland, ME: Stenhouse.

Helman, L. A. (2004). Building on the sound system of Spanish: Insights from the alphabetic spellings of English-language learners. *Reading Teacher, 57,* 452–460.

Hoonan, B. (2009). *ACTIVE* [Presentation handout]. Bainbridge Island, WA: Bainbridge Island School District.

Jiménez, R. T., García, G. E., & Pearson, P. D. (1996). The reading strategies of bilingual Latina/o students who are successful English readers: Opportunities and obstacles. *Reading Research Quarterly, 31,* 90–112.

Johnston, P. H. (2004). *Choice words: How our language affects children's learning*. Portland, ME: Stenhouse.

Keene, E. O., & Zimmerman, S. (1997). *Mosaic of thought: Teaching comprehension in a reader's workshop*. Portsmouth, NH: Heinemann.

Krashen, S. D. (1981). *Second language acquisition and second language learning*. New York: Pergamon Press.

Krashen, S. D. (1982). *Principles and practice in second language acquisition*. New York: Pergamon Press.

Krashen, S. D. (1994). Bilingual education and second language acquisition theory. In C. F. Leyba (Ed.), *Schooling and language minority students: A theoretical framework* (2nd ed., pp. 47–75). Los Angeles: Evaluation, Dissemination and Assessment Center, California State University.

Kuhl, P. K. (2004). Early language acquisition: Cracking the speech code. *Nature Reviews Neuroscience, 5,* 831-843.

Lenski, S. D., & Ehlers-Zavala, F. (2004). *Reading strategies for Spanish speakers*. Dubuque, IA: Kendall Hunt.

Leslie, L., & Caldwell, J. (2006). *Qualitative reading inventory-4* (4th ed.). Boston: Pearson/ Allyn and Bacon.

McGill-Franzen, A., & Allington, R. (2003, May-June). Bridging the summer reading gap. *Instructor, 112*(8). Retrieved from http://teacher.scholastic.com/products/instructor/ summer_reading.htm

Miramontes, O. B., Nadeau, A., & Commins, N. L. (1997). *Restructuring schools for linguistic diversity: Linking decision making to effective programs*. New York: Teachers College Press.

Moats, L. C. (2001). Overcoming the language gap. *American Educator, 25*(2), 5, 8–9.

Moje, E. B. (2006). Motivating texts, motivating contexts, motivating adolescents: An examination of the role of motivation in adolescent literacy practices and development. *Perspectives, 32*(3), 10–14.

Moll, L. C., Amanti, C., Neff, D., & González, N. (1992). Funds of knowledge for teaching: Using a qualitative approach to connect homes and classrooms. *Theory into Practice, 31*(2), 132–141.

Mooney, M. E. (1990). *Reading to, with, and by children.* Katonah, NY: Richard C. Owen.

Nagy, W. E. (1988). *Teaching vocabulary to improve reading comprehension.* Newark, DE: International Reading Association.

Paris, S. G., Wixson, K. K., & Palincsar, A. S. (1986). Instructional approaches to reading comprehension. In E. Z. Rothkopf (Ed.), *Review of research in education* (pp. 91–128). Washington, DC: American Educational Research Association.

Pearson, P. D., & Gallagher, M.C. (1983). The instruction of reading comprehension. *Contemporary Educational Psychology, 8,* 317–344.

Pennypacker, S. (2006). *Clementine.* New York: Hyperion Books for Children.

Reed, B., & Railsback, J. (2003). *Strategies and resources for mainstream teachers of English language learners.* Portland, OR: Northwest Regional Educational Laboratory.

Riddle Buly, M. (2006). Caught in the spell: Independent reading. In M. E. Mooney & T. A. Young (Eds.), *Caught in the spell of writing and reading: Grade 3 and beyond* (pp. 123–154). Katonah, NY: Richard C. Owen.

Riddle Buly, M., Coskie, T., Robinson, L., & Egawa, K. (2004). What is a literacy coach? (From the Coaches' Corner column). *Voices from the Middle, 12*(1), 60–61.

Robinson, L., & Riddle Buly, M. (2007). Breaking the language barrier: Promoting collaboration between general and special educators. *Teacher Education Quarterly, 34*(3), 83–94.

Rowling, J. K. (2003). *Harry Potter and the Order of the Phoenix.* New York: Scholastic.

Schmal, J. P. (2004). *Michoacán: A struggle for identity.* Retrieved from http://www .indigenouspeople.net/michoacan.htm

Slavin, R. E., & Cheung, A. (2004). How do English language learners learn to read? *Educational Leadership, 61*(6), 52–57.

Smith, M. W., & Wilhelm, J. D. (2002). *"Reading don't fix no Chevys": Literacy in the lives of young men.* Portsmouth, NH: Heinemann.

Suárez-Orozco, M., & Suárez-Orozco, C. (2003, March). *Immigration and education* [Three Lectures]. Invited lectures delivered to the East Hampton School District and the Ross Institute of New York. East Hampton, NY.

Taylor, B. M., Pressley, M. & Pearson, P. D. (2002). Research-supported characteristics of teachers and schools that promote reading achievement. In B. M. Taylor & P. D. Pearson (Eds.), *Teaching reading: Effective schools, accomplished teachers* (pp. 361–373). Mahwah, NJ: Erlbaum.

Thomas, W. P., & Collier, V. P. (2002). *A national study of school effectiveness for language minority students' long-term academic achievement.* Santa Cruz: Center for Research on Education, Diversity and Excellence, University of California. Retrieved from http://crede .berkeley.edu/research/llaa/1.1_final.html

Valencia, S. W., & Riddle Buly, M. (2004). Behind test scores: What struggling readers *really* need. *Reading Teacher, 57,* 520–531.

Vygotsky, L. S. (1978). *Mind in society: The development of higher psychological processes.* Cambridge, MA: Harvard University Press.

Author

Marsha **Riddle Buly** is proud to be a teacher who has had many opportunities in the educational arena. Included among these have been working as a reading specialist, ESL specialist, P–12 language arts coordinator, university professor, literacy coach, and board member of the growing Washington Association for Bilingual Education (WABE). Marsha started in the classroom and quickly realized she needed to know more about teaching reading. She became a reading specialist and then earned a doctorate focused on language learners and literacy, all the time returning to the classroom whenever possible.

Her journey, first as a mainstream classroom teacher with no experience working with language learners and a lack of knowledge about literacy instruction, provides a lens through which to address teachers' questions about how to teach the growing numbers of language learners they will meet in their literacy classrooms. The hours Marsha has spent and continues to spend in different K–8 classrooms provide valuable experience that enables her to share practical, manageable, research-based ideas that work.

This book was typeset in TheMix and Palatino by Precision Graphics.

Typefaces used on the cover include Slimbach Medium and Shannon Book.

The book was printed on 50-lb. Opaque Offset paper by Versa Press, Inc.

30% Total Recycled Fiber